Everyday Wellness for Women

Deborah Kern, Ph.D.

"Deborah Kern offers to all women a wisdom that comes only from those who have walked the path. As her teachers, she has made us continually aware of how the best teacher is always a student. Deborah is a masterful student of life who shares from her heart the gifts and knowledge she has gained through years of study and personal exploration. Her book is a beautiful expression of who she is."

Debbie and Carlos Rosas, Creators of The Nia Technique
(Neuromuscular Integrative Action)

"Gaining control over our minds is often the most difficult step in gaining control over our bodies. Deborah presents the key to understanding ourselves, our resistance and finally our successes to change our mindsets so we can change our bodies."

Cherie Boettcher, C.N.M, Director, Birth and Women's Center

"Deborah helped me prepare for one of the greatest challenges of my life-the climb at Mt.Kilimanjaro. Her lessons were many , her messages simple. Stay in the moment and don't forget to breathe. For a woman who moves 'at the speed of life', Deborah's grace, joy and giving are always in the present."

Kay Winzenried, Travel writer and photographer based in Dallas, Texas

Everyday Wellness for Women
Copyright 1999 by Deborah Kern, Ph.D.

Harmony Mind/Body Health
817-991-5835, www.DeborahKern.com

Cover design by Anthony Creative Services, 503-257-9885,
anthonycreative@worldnet.att.net
Photographs by Marianne Howard

First edition: February 1999

ISBN 0-9670440-0-6

Printed at Slaton Press, Moulton, Alabama

Contents

Dedicated to the three men in my life:
Lee, Jacob and Micah Slaton

Acknowledgments

So many people have supported me in the writing of this book I would like to thank:

Lee Slaton, my husband, for his loving support, great enthusiasm and for taking over childcare responsibilities when I needed a rest.

Lynn and Lee Kern, my parents, for teaching me by example how to work hard, care for others, feel the presence of God and enjoy life.

Jacob Slaton, my stepson, for teaching me the lesson of unconditional love and bringing the gifts of play, curiosity and laughter.

Micah Slaton, my baby son, for birthing a whole new side of myself and for his patience when mommy had to work at the computer.

Daliah Espinoza for lovingly caring for my children while I worked.

Cathleen Hill, my sister, for reading my manuscript many times over and cheering me on when I felt like giving up.

Debbie and Carlos Rosas for their endless support.

Sri Swami Satchidananda for his yoga teachings and his love.

Dr. Ed Tyska for generously sharing his immense knowledge in Ayurveda.

Shaina Noll and Jana Stanfield for inspiring me with their music.

All of my Nia and Yoga students for sharing of themselves and teaching me how to become a teacher.

Victor and Sounjalynne Mata for the use of their photography studio.

Marianne Howard for her talent as a photographer.

Paula Murphy Walter for sticking with me, nudging me on and editing this manuscript.

Jessica Hall Perez for her gift of Fire qualities and tireless dedication in reading and editing this manuscript.

Slaton Press for printing my book.

Mark Anthony for an inspired cover design.

INTRODUCTION

Initially, I began writing this book in response to the requests I received at my presentations. Ultimately, I wrote this book because I needed to hear the message! I truly believe the old adage: we teach what we need to learn.

When I began my journey in the health field in 1978, the focus was primarily on the physical aspects of health. I spent over eight years teaching patients how to lower their cholesterol, their blood pressure and their body fat, while telling them to increase their exercise levels. As a health educator, I was trained to inundate my patients with information about how to create these positive health changes without even acknowledging the possibility that their mental, emotional, social or spiritual being might be affecting their physical being. I was helping them create the image of a healthy woman. You know, a woman who looks the part - at least from the outside. She is thin, attractive, and well-dressed. She participates in every activity and eats all the right foods. She is perfect, and she follows all the rules. You have seen her, haven't you? Dr. William Carlyon describes her well in his poem, "The Healthiest Couple."

The Healthiest Couple
by William Carlyon

They brush and they floss
with care every day,
But not before breakfast
of both curds and whey,

He jogs for his heart
she bikes for her nerves;
They assert themselves daily
with appropriate verve.

He is loving and tender
and caring and kind,
Not one chauvinist thought
is allowed in his mind.

They are slim and attractive
well-dressed and just fun.
They are strong and well-immunized
against everything under the sun.

They are sparkling and lively
and having a ball.
Their diet? High fiber
and low cholesterol.

Cocktails are avoided
in favor of juice;
Cigarettes are shunned
as one would the noose;

They drive their car safely
with belts well in place;
At home not one hazard
ever will they face.

1.2 children they raise,
both sharing the job.
One is named Betty,
.2 is named Bob.

And when at the age of
two hundred and three,
They jog from this life
to one still more free,

They'll pass through those portals
to claim their reward,
And St. Peter will stop them
"just for a word."

"What Ho" he will say,
"You cannot go in .
This place is reserved
for those without sin."

"But, we've followed the rules"
she'll say with a fright.
"We're healthy" -
"Near perfect"-
"And incredibly bright."

"But, that's it" will say Peter,
drawing himself tall.
"You've missed the point of living
by thinking so small."

"Life is more than health habits,
though useful they be,
It is purpose and meaning,
the grand mystery."

"You've discovered a part
of what makes humans whole,
And mistaken that part
for the shape of the soul."

"You are fitter than fiddles
and sound as a bell,
Self-righteous, intolerant
and boring as hell."

First given to the "Promoting Health Through Schools
Conference", August 1980
William Carlyon, Ph.D., Adjunct Professor of Health Education,
University of New Mexico, Albuquerque.
Internet: 104203,3601@compuserv.com

In my desire to create the healthiest life, I too was attempting to be one of those women. I taught aerobics every day after work and competed in 10K races on the weekends. I monitored my fat intake and maintained a very low body fat percentage. I had the "right" house, the "right" job and participated in the "right" activities. But, when my husband told me he no longer wanted to be married, I was completely blind-sided. Why was I taken by surprise? Because I was so busy doing the "right" things that I was unaware of subtle changes in our relationship. Within three months, my marriage dissolved, I miscarried twins, and I resigned my position as a hospital department director. From the outside I appeared to be the perfect example of health, but from the inside I was unable to cope.

After spending the majority of my adult life trying to do the "right thing" I suddenly was at the bottom of the barrel. It was from this place of despair that I began to see a bigger message - a blessing in disguise. The difficult experiences ripped away all the false notions that I held so true and provided me a new understanding of life. This was when I realized that health was not just about looking great and having good blood chemistries - it was something much broader and deeper. My journey towards true health and wellness was emerging.

I returned to Dallas, my hometown, to go back to school and get my doctorate. Instead of studying what I already "knew", I decided to study how other cultures created health. I learned as much as I could about Chinese medicine, Ayurveda and Yoga. I lived on an ashram and experienced a yogic lifestyle. I lived in the rainforest of Costa Rica and studied herbal medicine with a group of indigenous women. As I flooded myself with experiences that were quite different from what I once considered the "right" health practices, my life began to shift and my soul began to heal. It was this shift that put me on a new course in life. A course that has given me a deeper understanding of the challenges that women face today as we try to find time for ourselves and our wellness.

After completing my doctorate, I found myself juggling my new marriage, a 7-year-old stepson and a full-time director position at a Mind/Body Wellness Center. Within three years, I decided to resign my position, start my own speaking business and prepare for the birth of my first son. At 40, a whole new set of circumstances was once again upon my life. Between nursing a baby, cooking for a family, checking 4th grade homework, going for days without sleep, maintaining my speaking business and dealing with the aftereffects of pregnancy, I finally understood what thousands of women, with whom I have worked, claim. They just didn't have time to exercise, eat right or meditate - they didn't have time for themselves. Like all of those women I felt like life had become a roller coaster. I wrote this book to share some of the ways that I have learned to create wellness while riding the roller coaster of life.

I am excited to share what I've learned with you, but I must admit I procrastinated writing this book. Why? I doubted my worth. I wanted to wait until I had time to make it "perfect" - until life settled down. I postponed the pictures while I was pregnant- and then until I could lose the postpartum weight. Finally, I realized that this procrastination was a perfect metaphor for life. If you wait for conditions to be "perfect" before you're willing to move forward, you will never move forward. So, I took the leap. I wrote in my "spare" moments and had photos taken, just as I am, hoping that you will be inspired to take the leap and do things you've been postponing, too.

I've entitled the book _Everyday Wellness for Women_ because I trust it will provide ideas and philosophies that you can implement into your everyday life. Chapter 1 is an overview of the mind/body connection and general health - topics I am often asked to present. Chapter 2 will help you learn a new way of understanding your individual nature. I suggest that you read the first two chapters in order, and then chose any and all of the chapters that interest you.

If you find that you would really like to delve into any of the topics more deeply, I have provided a resource list at the end of each chapter.

Enjoy your journey.........

Chapter I
Creating Health
Through Mind/Body Connection

Many people believe that mind and body are separate entities. In part, this belief comes from the feeling that they are split. For instance, have you ever had the experience of driving down the highway mulling over some problem or thinking about some future event? Suddenly you realize you've missed your exit and you wonder how in the world you got so far down the road - you don't even remember passing the usual landmarks. We've all had this kind of experience. You might believe that your mind and body live in separate worlds, one not affecting the other, but this is a myth. Mind and body are one. Anything affecting your mind instantly affects your body, and anything affecting your body instantly affects your mind.

Most traditional medical systems not only acknowledge the mind/body connection, but also make use of its extraordinary power. Western medicine, however, has regarded the mind and body as separate entities and has ignored the power of their interconnectedness. The concept of mind and body as separate entities was established in the 17th century. Originally it permitted medical science the freedom to explore and experiment on the body while preserving the domain of the mind for

1

the church. As medicine evolved over the next three centuries, its focus on the body provided many discoveries about the nature and treatment of disease states. Unfortunately, this narrow focus has also obscured the importance of the interactions between mind and body and overshadowed the importance of the mind in producing and alleviating disease.

During the past 30 years, there has been a powerful scientific movement to explore these interactions. Research shows that when people tap into the power of the mind/body connection, they not only have a better understanding of the sources of stress, but they can also reduce the stress more easily and effectively. This stress reduction occurs by quieting the mind and using it to mobilize the body to heal itself. This mind/body approach is forming the basis for a new perspective on medicine and healing in which mind/body interactions are used to enhance health care.

Mind/Body Experience

Try this: raise your arm up and down twenty times while thinking about all of the tasks you need to get done by the end of the day. Now notice how you are breathing, and notice how you are feeling. Stressed, rushed, and out of breath.

Now raise the other arm up and down, but this time, imagine that you are placing a teacup on a high shelf. As you reach to set the cup on the shelf, inhale deeply. Then as you lower your arm, exhale. Reach up again to get the cup, inhaling as you raise your arm. Bring the cup back down as you exhale. Do this 20 times.

Now notice how you are feeling. Relaxed, meditative, and peaceful.

Both activities required that you raise and lower your arm twenty times, but the feelings they created were very different. Why? Because you cannot separate mind and body. When your mind is stressed and rushed, your body becomes tense and movement is restricted. When your mind is relaxed and calm, your body becomes relaxed and movement is fluid.

How did we get so stressed?

During the past 100 years, our bodies have not changed genetically. But the world in which we live has dramatically changed. According to psychologists Joel and Michelle Levy, we have to make more decisions and process more information in one day than our ancestors did in a year! Think about it. One hundred years ago people did not have telephones, television, radio, fax, e-mail, cars, cash machines or fast food restaurants. Their pace of life was much, much slower. To a housewife a hundred years ago, what was Monday? Wash day. A whole day for nothing but laundry. No decisions. Lots of physical activity, though. Just the opposite of our lives today, where Monday represents a myriad of chores that need to be accomplished in a short amount of time, but rarely does it represent much physical activity.

So when the surgeon general says that 70-85 percent of all major illness is directly linked to lifestyle, I used to think that meant diet, exercise and smoking. Now I believe it is something deeper than health behaviors. I believe that we are having coping difficulties with the

3

pace and chaos of our lives. It is the relentless pace and sense of disconnection that manifests unhealthy behaviors, like overeating, alcohol or drug use, or (my personal favorite) being overcomitted to doing so many "things" that you have no time to feel. If we ever want to truly heal, we must shift our focus from the result of behaviors, such as high blood pressure, overweight, chronic fatigue or migraine headaches, and look at the cause of the coping difficulties.

We need to stop bashing ourselves for the behaviors that we don't like, take a step back, and ask "what is causing these behaviors?". We need to stop punishing ourselves and find ways to take care of ourselves.

The Fight-or-Flight: The First Response to Stress

As human beings have evolved over thousands of years, they have developed a physcial and biochemical response to acute stress, or danger, that Dr. Walter Cannon called the "fight-or-flight" response. The fight-or-flight response does just what it sounds like: when you are threatened, it prepares the body to flee or to fight because you are in a state of emergency. The instant you perceive danger your heart beats faster and pumps with greater force, and your blood pressure rapidly elevates. Blood supply is shunted away from the digestive system to the large muscles, and your lungs respond by delivering more oxygen to muscle tissue. Simultaneously, powerful adrenalinelike chemicals flood your body so that you have the speed and force to survive. Whether fleeing from a saber-toothed tiger or fighting an intruder, this ability to fight or flee for life has been necessary for our survival as a species.

4

Stress and Survival in a Modern World

The fight-or-flight response is the first reaction to stress. The second response is "chronic vigilance." This is when the body prepares for long-term challenge. Among our early ancestors, this type of challenge was often lack of food sources or a long search for a dry, warm place to live. During chronic vigilance the stress hormone "cortisol" rises. In response, blood pressure slowly rises; metabolism drops and gastric acid increases to maximize the caloric expenditure. High-energy fats and blood clotting agents are released into your bloodstream where energy is diverted from your immune system, and "nonessentials," such as sex hormones, are dramatically suppressed.

For most of us, stress does not come from real physical danger or environmental deprivation. Nevertheless, our bodies react to stress as if it were the saber-toothed tiger or a threat of starvation. Daily challenges such as traffic, completing a project, caring for a family, or even competing in leisure activities can trigger a cascade of inappropriate and potentially damaging physiological and biochemical responses.

Dr. Walter Cannon and Dr. Hans Selye showed that, affected by the stress response, chain reactions of hormones either enhanced or suppressed immune function. For instance, corticosteroid hormones are produced when a person is feeling stressed. These hormones suppress immune function. They also prompt mood changes, especially depression. Both mind and body are affected.

Mind/Body Communication

Stress hormones are not the only form of mind/body communication. From the groundbreaking discoveries of Candace Pert, Ph.D. and her colleagues, we now know that every thought we have is communicated throughout the body via chemical messengers called neuropeptides, or molecules of emotion. These molecules are produced in the brain when you have a thought or emotion and then received by cells all over the body. But the communication is not just a transmission, brain to the body - it is two-way communication. The cells in the organs produce the very same chemicals the brain does, when you are thinking or feeling emotions.

What this means is that if you are anxious or worried about how you're going to pay your credit card bill, chemicals such as epinephrine, norepinephrine, and cortisol are produced. When the cells in the immune system receive these chemicals, immune function is impaired. T-cell production and natural killer cell activity slows down. On the other hand, if you are full of joy and contentment, chemicals such as favorable interferons and interleukins are produced. When cells in the immune system receive these chemicals, immune function is boosted. T-cell production and natural killer cell activities increase. In a very real way, your immune system is paying attention to what you are thinking. Not only do immune cells receive messages from the brain via neuropeptides, but they also produce the very same neuropeptides the brain produces.

What does this mean? As an example, let's look at natural killer cells. These are the cells in the immune system that are responsible for attacking and destroying can-

6

cerous tumors. All of us produce mutated and aberrant cells every day, but most of the time the natural killer cells do their jobs very well and don't allow tumors to grow; therefore, so we don't become ill. But if the natural killer cells are interrupted by the flow of neuropeptides caused by emotions of anger, fear or worry, they can't do their jobs adequately.

At this point it is important to clarify that I am not saying that people cause their cancer with their thoughts. What I am saying is that their thoughts have a powerful effect on how well their immune system works.

The brain and the immune system are not the only places where neuropeptides and receptors are found. Dr. Pert and her partner, Michael Ruff, Ph.D. discovered that the entire lining of the intestines contains neuropeptides and receptors. In fact, Dr. Pert asserts that "it seems entirely possible to me that the density of receptors in the intestines may be why we feel our emotions in that part of the anatomy, often referring to them as 'gut feelings.'"
And what is the typical response in our culture to a "gut feeling"? We pull out a piece of paper and draw a line down the middle of it, and list the pros on one side and the cons on the other side. We may have had a gut feeling NOT to do something, but if the pros outweigh the cons, we know that "logically" we should do it. Then, a week or a month or a year later we say to ourselves, "I knew I shouldn't have done that!" That's because the gut is probably more accurate than analytical thought, because it doesn't doubt itself.

How does this apply to you?

Women have always known through their own intuition that stress can wreak havoc in our bodies. Supporting our intuition is three decades of research which shows that stress can overstimulate the heart, create imbalances in hormonal output and suppress immune function. Now, at a time when women seem to be more stressed than ever, the need for understanding the mind/body connection - both for the prevention and treatment of common conditions- could not be greater.

My goal is to remind you what you already know deep in your heart. Women know that the interweaving relationships between mind, body, spirit, emotions, environment, relationships and occupation create who we are. And I'd like to share with you some simple ways to help you re-connect to your own inner wisdom.

Move Your Body

It is now common knowledge that we all need to exercise our bodies in order to stay well. We need cardiovascular exercise to keep our hearts and lungs healthy, strength exercises to maintain good posture and prevent osteoporosis, and flexibility exercises to stay pliable, graceful and comfortable in our bodies. But many of us have fallen prey to the myth that we must go to a gym to exercise or engage in a minimum of thirty, uninterrupted minutes, in order to get any benefit. That just isn't true. What we really need to do is put movement back into our daily lives.

If we go through our days without releasing muscular tension, we expose ourselves to a life of aches, pains and very little energy. Chapter 3 gives suggestions for ways to add movement back into your life in order to heal those aches and pains and revitalize yourself.

Nourishment: How to Feed Hungry Body and Mind

"Eat more carbohydrate and less protein." "Eat more protein and less carbohydrate." "Eat nothing after 8:00 pm." You are what you eat. Not only does our food intake affect our physical wellbeing; but also our mental and emotional, as well. Chemicals released in foods actually change our emotional and mental state. Chapter 4 will help you learn how to trust your internal guidance for food choices. By learning how foods affect your moods, you will be able to proactively choose snacks and meals.

Your Body Believes Every Word You Say

How powerful are your thoughts? So powerful that in studies of patients with Multiple Personality Disorder it has been shown that when one personality is present the patient needs glasses to see; however, when another personality surfaces the patient has perfect visual acuity. Also, when one personality is present the patient is an insulin dependent diabetic, but when another personality emerges, the patient is metabolically normal.

The mind's affect on the body is so powerful that Chapter 5 is devoted to techniques to help you take a look at what your mind is habitually doing- and help you create mental habits that are healing in nature.

Body Image: In the Eye of the Beholder

Some of the most common thoughts among women are negative thoughts about our bodies. Why? Mainly because our culture holds an ideal of beauty that very few women can maintain without tremendous time, effort, cosmetics and surgery. Chapter 6 is devoted to body image because it is important for women to understand how strong the cultural influence has been on our perceptions of ourselves.

Breath: The Power to Return to Center

Your breath is one of the best tools at your disposal for learning about the mind/body connection and for consciously shifting from a stress response to a relaxed response. It is also a tangible connection to your spirit. The word spirit comes from the Latin root "spiritus" which means breath.

In Chapter 7 you can learn several breathing techniques that will help you connect to your spirit and begin to untie the knots - emotional and physical.

Simplify Your Life

Because our life patterns are so deeply ingrained, my first recommendation is to simplify your life. One of the reasons it is so hard to find the source that is driving our behaviors is that we are addicted to complexity. Women, especially, are masters at doing ten things at once. So when we have a chance to sit quietly, we feel guilty or anxious. Therefore, we don't ever sit quietly - which means we don't really know what might be at the source of our discomforts. Not to mention the fact that many of us say we would love to exercise and eat right - but we just don't have time. Our lives have become so complicated!

Simplifying your life is a vital step in re-connecting mind, body and spirit; therefore, I have devoted the entirety of Chapter 8 to this subject.

Meditation: Calming a Stormy Mind

Studies have shown that the average person has about 60,000 thoughts per day, and that 90% of the thoughts you have today are the same ones you had yesterday. If you are even close to average, this means that your mind is constantly chattering. Most people are aware this chatter is disturbing their "peace of mind", but they can't seem to stop it. This is where the practice of meditation comes into use. It not only helps you stop the chatter, but it can strengthen your focus and concentration. And once the mind stops disturbing the body, the body functions much better. In Chapter 9 you can learn some simple meditation techniques to practice that will help you quiet your mind and stop the chattering.

Daily Massage: The Healing Power of Touch

Everyone needs to be touched. But in America there aren't many socially acceptable, nonsexual forms of touch. So most of us are "touch deprived." Many of us don't have the time or the money to get a massage every day. However, most of us rub a cramped foot or bashed hand. This instinct to touch or rub a hurt spot is a good one. In Chapter 10 you will learn a self-massage technique that will help you receive the benefits of massage on a daily basis.

As you read the following chapters, I hope that you find some practical and usable suggestions to help you create more health and happiness in your life. My desire is to share with you my experiences, not give you a "prescription" for living, so please remember that although I offer many activities for you to try, the ultimate guide comes from inside of you.

Resources:

Northrup, Christiane. (1994) Women's Bodies, Women's Wisdom. Bantam Books.

Pert, Candace. (1997) Molecules of Emotion. Scribner.

Alternative Medicine: Expanding Medical Horizons. A Report to the National Institutes of Health on Alternative Medical Systems and Practices in the United States. Document # 017-040-00537-7.
To order call: 202-512-1800.

Chapter II
You are Unique:
Learning Your Mind/Body Type

"There is a vitality, a life force, an energy, a quickening, that is translated through you into action, and because there is only one of you in all time, this expression is unique. And if you block it, it will never exist through any other medium and will be lost."
Martha Graham

We all have a unique nature: a unique body type, a unique personality, and unique strengths and weaknesses. Why do we try to all fit into the same box? How sad that many of us spend precious life energy trying to change the nature with which we are blessed!

Can you recall the first time you wanted to change something about your body? The earliest memory I have of being dissatisfied with my body comes from first grade. I vividly remember loving to dance and swirl my skirts - and how excited I was to take my first ballet class. But when the elegant, French ballet teacher shamed me in front of everyone by saying that I was "much too large to dance," I was crushed. It was then that I became aware that something was wrong with my body size. From that day forward I tried everything I could to become smaller. As fate would have it, my younger sister was everything

I wanted to be: petite, shapely, blonde-haired and blue-eyed. We shared a bathroom, so as we brushed our hair to get ready for school, I would stand behind her (since I was much taller) and curse my thick wavy brown hair - longing for her straight blond hair and wishing to be as petite as she.

The irony is that the whole time that I was wishing to have her body and her hair, she was wishing to have mine!! It is also ironic that now, at 40 years old, my favorite activity is dancing. Have you ever spent time and energy trying to look like someone else? If so, I hope this chapter helps you realize what a waste of time and energy it is!

You probably learned in your middle school health class that three body types exist: ectomorph - the thin, petite build; mesomorph - the medium, muscular build; and endomorph - the fleshy, stocky build. This information is widely accepted in the health science field. But it is interesting that although we recognize the predisposition for people to be uniquely different in body type, we as women, spend most of our lives trying to be thin mesomorphs. This means that two-thirds of us are constantly trying to force ourselves into an unnatural state that is either thinner or more muscular than our own natural build. We waste precious life energy dieting, overexercising, and having plastic surgeries to only bring about feelings of shame, embarrassment and guilt.

Ayurveda: The Science of Life

Although I began working on my poor body image in my early 30's, it wasn't until I discovered Ayurveda, the ancient healing system from India, that I truly began to heal. The Ayurvedic health system identifies the specific physical and psychological differences in individuals. Physical (thin, solid, dark or pale), mental (quick-witted, thoughtful or good memory), emotional (high strung, temperamental or calm) and social characteristics (talkative, loyal or generous) can be identified and then classified into three distinct mind/body types. In Sanskrit, the ancient language of India, the three mind/body types are called Vata, Pitta, and Kapha. But to make things easier to understand I have re-named them for this book as Air, Fire and Earth.

The following questionnaire is designed to help you determine your mind/body type and how it is expressed in your physical, emotional and mental self. You will immediately notice that the questionnaire is brief and highly subjective. That's because it is designed to help you learn more about yourself, not to label you. When answering the questions, please place a check beside the answer that best describes your nature. In other words, the answer that best describes the general patterns of your life, not just how you have been feeling lately. If you absolutely can't make up your mind, you may check more than one or leave the item blank. When you have completed the questions, total the number of checks in each of the columns.

This questionnaire is not intended to precisely and accurately diagnose or label you. It is meant to give you an idea of your tendencies and areas of dominance. If you were to visit an Ayurvedic physician, you would fill out a much lengthier questionnaire and have a one-hour interview and pulse diagnosis with the physician to determine your mind/body type.

Body/Mind Type Questionnaire

Please check the response that best describes you:

1. Hair texture
___A. dry, curly, full of body
___B. straight, fine
___C. thick, wavy, shiny

2. Hair color
___A. medium or light brown
___B. blond or reddish tone or early gray
___C. dark brown, black

3. Skin texture
___A. on the dry side
___B. delicate, sensitive
___C. oily, smooth

4. Complexion (when compared to others of same race)
___A. darker
___B. more reddish, freckled
___C. lighter

5. Bone size
___A. small
___B. average
___C. large

6. Eyes

___A. small

___ B. medium

___C. large

7. Weight

___A. thin, hard to gain

___B. average

___C. heavy, easy to gain

8. Run like a

___A. deer

___B. tiger

___C. bear

9. Energy level

___A. fluctuates, to come in waves

___B. is moderate or high, can push myself too hard

___C. is steady

10. Preferred climate

___A. dislike cold; am comfortable in warm and hot weather

___B. dislike heat; perspire easily; thrive in winter

___C. dislike damp cold, tolerate extremes well

11. Typical hunger level

___A. can vary from excessive to no interest in food

___B. is intense, I need regular meals

___C. is usually low but can be emotionally driven

12. Sleep pattern

___A. interrupted, light

___B. sound, moderate

___C. deep, long; am slow to awaken

17

13. Typical dreams

___A. flying, looking down at the ground, jumping, chase scenes

___B. fire, violence, anger

___C. oceans, clouds, romance

14. Sexual interest

___A. strong when romantically involved, low to moderate otherwise

___B. moderate to strong

___C. slow to awaken, but sustained; generally strong

15. Most sensitive to

___A. noise

___B. bright light

___C. strong odors

16. Emotional moods

___A. change easily, very responsive

___B. quick-tempered, intense

___C. even-tempered, slow to anger

17. Reaction to stress

___A. anxious, fearful

___B. irritated

___C. mostly calm

18. Spending habits

___A. am easy and impulsive

___B. am careful, but I spend

___C. tend to save, accumulate

19. Mental activity
___A. quick mind, restless
___B. sharp intellect, aggressive
___C. calm, steady, stable

20. Preferred learning style
___A. listening to a speaker
___B. reading or using visual aids
___C. associating it with another memory

21. Memory
___A. short term best
___B. good overall
___C. long term best

22. Manner of speaking
___A. fast and often excessive
___B. clear, precise; detailed
___C. soothing, slow, with moments of silence

23. Most outstanding trait
___A. vivacious
___B. determined
___C. easy going

24. Friendships
___A. easily adapt to different kinds of people
___B. often choose friends on the basis of their values
___C. am slow to make new friends but forever loyal

25. Friends and family say I should be more
___A. settled
___B. tolerant
___C. enthusiastic

TOTALS:
Add all of the A, B and C responses and place the total in the space provided.

(A) AIR

_____

(B) FIRE

_____

(C) EARTH

_____

All of us have some air, some fire and some earth. But our "recipes" are different. For instance, my two most dominant characteristics are air and earth, and I have very little fire in my nature. The goal is not to have a balance of each of the characteristics (that would be the same mistake as making everyone be the same body type), but the goal is to keep each of the characteristics you express in its balanced state.

As you read about the characteristics of each of the three mind/body types you will find that some of them fit you very well and others don't. You may find that mentally you express one characteristic and physically you express another, or that your skin and hair express one while your digestion and energy level express another. This is perfectly normal. What's important is that you begin tuning into your self and noticing how you feel when you are balanced and when you are "not quite yourself".

Air in Balance

Air is associated with lightness, quickness and dryness. A woman who has dominant Air, and in her balanced and healthy state, is light, imaginative, joyous, sensitive, creative, quick-minded, exhilarated and spontaneous. When a woman with a dominant Air nature is in balance, she has an abundance of quick energy, but may tire easily. She is often very funny and charming, she tends to interrupt the conversation and then forgets what she wanted to say; however, you forgive her because you know it's completely unintentional.

Causes for Air Out of Balance

* stress (time or financial pressures, relationship
        problems, worry about loved ones...)
* physical exhaustion or mental strain
* alcohol or drug addiction (including cigarettes)
* sudden change (seasons, travel, moving, marriage /
        divorce...)
* a diet of raw, cold, dry foods
* habitually skipping meals
* going without sleep
* emotional suffering (grief, fear or unexpected shock)
* cold, dry weather

Air Out of Balance

When out of balance, the Air woman's quick mind begins to move so quickly that it spins uncontrollably, preventing her from completing a thought - let alone a project. This makes her forgetful and keeps her awake at night, even though her body is exhausted. Then, as her mind continues to spin, she begins to feel worried, anxious and fearful. She often forgets to eat - which makes her feel even more "light headed" and "spacey". In her physical body, she often experiences spasms, chills, shakiness, constipation or gas.

Restoring Balance to Air

* regular habits
* quiet
* rest
* warmth
* steady nourishment
* meditation

To stay in balance, it is very important for Air women to be regular in life (keeping a regular schedule for meals, sleeping, and other needed activities), and to compensate for a relative lack of stability in the body's functioning. Rest and warmth are also essential in keeping Air balanced. But probably the most significant practice for an Air woman to maintain is the practice of calming the mind. That is why meditation and relaxation are vital parts of this woman's healthy lifestyle (see Chapter 9).

Susan's Story

One of my clients, Susan*, was a typical Air type. When she filled out the questionnaire all but three of the check marks fell into the Air category. She was a petite, vivacious and outgoing woman who worked in sales. All of the clients loved her. In fact, they ONLY wanted to work with her when placing an order. As the business grew Susan hired new staff to help with the growing demands. Unfortunately, her workload continued to increase as she felt compelled to serve the clients who demanded her involvement. She began to come in early and work through her lunch break, just to meet the increased workload. Her weight began to drop, and she was feeling very anxious. Her anxiety prevented her from sleeping at night, even though she was exhausted from her work.

When she first came to see me, Susan was taking tranquilizers and seeing a psychologist twice a week. She was overwhelmed with life. She said she felt like a hamster in a cage, endlessly running on a wheel and never getting anywhere. It was clear that the nature of her job was pushing her Air nature out of balance. Although the creativity and the contact with people was satisfying her, the relentless pace and the overcrowded, noisy office were driving her out of balance.

To help her become more balanced so she could view her situation more clearly, I recommended that Susan take the following steps:
1. Eat several small warm meals throughout the day.
2. Practice deep breathing at least 3 times a day.
   (see Chapter 7)

23

3. Make things as quiet as possible in her car and her home.
4. Do not watch the news before going to bed.
5. Take a warm bath and drink Chamomile tea an hour before going to bed.
6. Turn out the lights by 10:00 p.m.
7. Do progressive muscle relaxation in bed before falling asleep.
8. Practice 20 minutes of meditation in the early morning. (see Chapter 9)

After practicing these suggestions for two weeks, Susan felt much better. She was able to stop taking her medication, and she began to think clearly enough in her therapy sessions to make decisions about how to make changes in her life. Well-rested and clear-headed, she made the decision to change jobs. Within a month, she was back to her cheerful, enthusiastic self.

Fire in Balance

A Fire woman in balance is often courageous, clearheaded, successful, enterprising, joyous, competitive and sharp minded. She has a medium build with hair that is reddish, graying or balding (the ancient wisdom says that because the fire is so hot it either turns the hair red, burns the color out or burns the hair off the top of the head!). A Fire dominant woman is intense and has a strong digestion. She is very articulate, decisive, efficient, and organized. She has a good sense of judgment and critical thinking skills.

Causes for Fire out of Balance

* stress to which you have reacted with suppressed anger, frustration, and resentment
* excessive demands on yourself or on others
* too much spicy or fried food or alcoholic beverages
* hot, humid weather
* heat-fatigue or sunburn
* unmet hunger needs

Fire Out of Balance

Out of balance, Fire often turns a sharp mind into a sharp tongue, good judgment into judgmentalism, and critical thinking into simply critical. The out of balance Fire woman becomes easily frustrated and irritated, and may find herself becoming fanatical about organization and perfection. She may become so focused on achieving a goal that she overworks herself and allows no time for relaxation and rejuvenation.

Restoring Balance to Fire

* coolness
* leisure and unstructured schedule
* timely meals
* non-competitive activities
* let go of the need to have things go the way you think they should go
* practice being non-judgmental
* don't compare

Vivian's Story

Vivian* was a clinical assistant in a large plastic surgery office. Because she was so enterprising and organized, she developed new systems for the inventory of products. She was always informed on the latest developments in the field of skin care due to her love of knowledge. So it was no surprise when she was promoted to a management position.

Unfortunately, this meant that she would now have to deal face-to-face with a cumbersome bureaucracy. Although the plans and ideas she developed would have helped increase business at the clinic, most of them "died" in committee. This left Vivian feeling more and more frustrated. Meanwhile, because of her new responsibilities Vivian often missed her lunch - or had to delay lunch by an hour or two.

When Vivian came to see me she was exhibiting signs of suppressed anger, and feeling constantly irritable and annoyed. She had begun to lash out at fellow employees with criticisms and anger. At 48, she was just beginning to experience the hormonal changes of menopause, and her hot flashes suddenly increased in intensity and frequency.

For Vivian the solution was simple, but not easy. I recommended that she begin packing a lunch every day so she could eat when she was hungry. However, the main cause of her imbalance was the anger she felt when her ideas and plans were not accepted and carried out. This is very common for women with dominant fire. Their sharp minds and good organizational skills help them develop excellent strategies, but when people don't follow their plan, they become very irritated. They must let go of the need to have things go the way they think they should go. This is not what Vivian wanted to hear. For months she stayed at that job, unable to let go of having things go the way she wanted - and for months, her symptoms worsened. Finally, she left her position. She joined a much smaller company where her ideas were not only appreciated, they were needed. In this environment, where she had more autonomy, Vivian flourished and her out-of-balance symptoms disappeared.

Earth in Balance

A woman who is dominant Earth is strong, steady, wise, serene, and earthy. She has strong bones, strong teeth, and the capability of storing energy - which may result in a well-proportioned, heavier body. She is often voluptuous with beautiful large eyes, and she is compassionate and calm. In her healthy state, Earth gives the qualities of being forgiving, deliberate, and able to save money and keep friends. Earth women are often unflappable and very loyal.

Causes for Earth Out of Balance

* reacting to stress by sleeping or overeating
* overeating sugar, salt, or dairy products
* reacting to stress by withdrawing
* strong emphasis on possessing, storing, and saving
    things
* dependant or overprotective relationships
* cold, damp weather

Earth Out of Balance

Out of balance, however, the slow, steady nature can become so slow it gets stuck. The body continues to store fluids or fat. Emotionally the woman clings to possessions and relationships that she needs to release. Instead of spinning out of control like Air or flaring out a hot temper like Fire, Earth out of balance becomes lethargic and depressed.

Restoring Balance to Earth

* get out and be with friends
* regular exercise
* seek variety
* weight control
* warmth and dryness
* reduce sweet heavy foods
* reduce dairy products
* routinely clean out clutter

Karen's Story

Karen* owns a quaint restaurant that specializes in European cuisine. After her business partner had a stroke, she found herself managing the workload of two people while her partner recuperated. Luckily, Karen's dominant Earth nature provided her with the stamina to work long hours, as well as the compassion to help nurture her partner back to health. However, the emotional shock of her partner's sudden illness combined with the anxiety of keeping the business alive, drove Karen to the refrigerator, freezer or pantry late at night to soothe herself. After a couple of months of nightly food indulgences, Karen put on 20 pounds. Now, instead of getting out of bed to do her early morning walk, she was hitting the snooze on her alarm clock. She began to feel lethargic all day long. By the time she came to see me, she was very depressed about her weight gain. She felt hopeless.

Balancing earth is pretty straight forward: Lighten up and get moving! The first thing I suggested for Karen was to find a way to move around more throughout the day. Her days were spent mostly sitting at a desk, talking on the phone or working at the computer, while her nights were spent greeting guests and overseeing restaurant operations. Of course her first reaction was to say that she just didn't have time to exercise until her partner was well - and she was right. She absolutely didn't have time to go to a gym, change clothes, take a class or walk on a treadmill, shower and drive back to work. But she did have time to wake up 20 minutes earlier than she had been and ride her exercise bike before showering for the day. And she did have time to walk for 20 minutes during her lunch hour. Once she added this bit of activity into her days she immediately began feeling better. It was easier for her to resist eating heavy lunches knowing that she was getting ready for a walk, and the walk gave her just the boost she needed to make it past her normal 3 p.m. candy bar and soft drink. She lost some weight, but more importantly she felt energized and hopeful again.

How to use this information:

All of us have a combination of Air, Fire and Earth in our nature. And all of us can go out of balance in any one of the three areas - but it's most likely that we will go out of balance in the area that is our dominant nature. Here are six questions to ask yourself to see if you are in or out of balance:

1. Do I eat when I'm hungry and stop when I'm full?
2. Do I have plenty of energy for my day?
3. Do I sleep well at night?
4. Are my relationships good?
5. Is my elimination good?
6. Am I generally peaceful and joyous?

These are the six questions I ask myself, and I have my clients ask themselves, to determine if they are in or out of balance. If you answer no to any one of the questions, then ask yourself if it feels like Air, Fire or Earth that is out of balance. Then take the appropriate steps to bring that element back into balance. Many times you will feel that one element is out of balance, and when you take steps to bring it back into balance you suddenly feel that another one is out of balance. Just keep taking the necessary steps to bring them into balance. It is an ongoing process.

If you want more information on specifics of diet, herbs, and therapies try reading one of the books from the following reference list.

Resources:

Chopra, Deepak (1991) Perfect Health. Harmony Books

Douillard, John   (1994) Body, Mind and Sport. Crown Trade Paperbacks.

Frawley, David (1990) Ayurvedic Healing. Passage Press.

Frawley, David, and Lad, Vasant (1986) The Yoga of Herbs. Lotus Press.

Lad, Vasant. (1984) Ayurveda: The Science of Self-Healing Lotus Press.

Lonsdorf, Nancy, Butler, Veronica, and Brown, Melanie (1995) A Woman's Best Medicine: Health Happiness, and Long Life Through Ayur-Veda. Los Angeles: Jeremy Tarcher.

* The names used for each case study are fictitious.

Chapter III
Move Your Body

3 goals of exercise
1. To rejuvenate the body and cultivate the mind
2. To remove stress
3. To develop mind-body coordination
John Douillard, Mind, Body and Sport

Move your body

Exercise can be intimidating. I have vivid memories of being the slowest 50-yard dasher and the last to be picked for a team in "capture the flag". It was humiliating. So when I found out that being in the high school band would exempt me from physical education classes, I was delighted! It probably won't surprise you that I chose a college that did not have a Physical Education requirement. Unfortunately, by the time I graduated from college I had become very sedentary. Following college, I worked as an au pair in France for nine months and returned to start graduate school thirty pounds heavier than when I had left. The combination of a sedentary lifestyle and freshly baked "pain au chocolat" was devastating to my physical, emotional and energetic condition.

As soon as the first semester of graduate school began, I realized I had to do something because I felt so sluggish and lethargic that I was having a hard time staying awake in class. At that time in 1980 jogging was very popular, so I tried it. And I hated it! With each pounding step I could feel my brain jarring against my skull. I gasped for breath and my sides ached. I was embarrassed to be seen and was just plain bored. Luckily, aerobic dance was just beginning to be available as a form of exercise and I joined my first class. I loved the music and the fun of dancing around with other people. I was instantly hooked! The physical conditioning and stress release gave me more energy, so I began teaching aerobic dance within six months. For the next ten years I enjoyed teaching several varieties of aerobic dance: high impact, low impact, and step. I also discovered that I had a natural ability for racewalking and began racing on the weekends.

When "Fitness" Isn't Healthy

By 1990, however, I was feeling the stress of having to look a certain way in my leotard, plus my joints were feeling the stress of overuse. In order to maintain the very low body fat I considered "ideal", I was constantly restricting my calories and was exercising for at least two hours a day, seven days a week. What started out as a healthy lifestyle change had become an obsession. I used exercise as a way to punish my body when I had been "bad" by eating ice cream or pizza. And I used exercise as a way to numb myself from feeling emotions that I wanted to avoid.

Fortunately, I happened to attend a session during an aerobics convention that changed my view of fitness altogether. This movement technique changed not only my view of fitness, but also my life. It is called Nia, which stands for Neuromuscular Integrative Action.

Nia: A Holistic Approach to Fitness

Nia is a cardiovascular exercise program that uses movements based on principles and techniques from Tai Chi, Tae Kwon Do, Aikido, Jazz, Modern Dance, Duncan Dance, Body Integration Therapies and Yoga. Studying Nia, however, is much more than an exercise class. It is a lifestyle that promotes self-directed, healthy choices in movement, nutrition, relationships, and all aspects of life. Nia fosters healthy self-esteem, intuition and communication skills. It teaches you how to enjoy being in your body and how to get the most from your body. And, most importantly, it provides a healing experience for mind, body, emotions and spirit. At the end of this chapter you will find information on how to contact the Nia office to find a teacher in your area or to find out how to become a certified teacher. Don't hesitate. Go experience Nia for yourself!

Creating a Nia Experience in Your Daily Life

One of the concepts that we practice in Nia is moving through life "aware". Being aware is quite different from simply being awake. When you are aware of your body you can constantly do movements that help release tension, or strengthen or energize it. For instance, most people wake up and plug through the morning with low energy levels or caffeine-stimulated energy. By being aware of your body you can change this pattern. When you wake up in the morning, before you even move an inch, take a minute to breathe deeply. Breath is the beginning of all movement.

While still in bed, roll over onto your belly and push yourself onto all fours. Sit back onto your heels (this is called "child's pose" in yoga). Take a moment to breathe deeply and stretch your lower back. Then stand up beside your bed and stretch your arms overhead as you take in a deep breath. When you exhale, bend forward and let your head hang. Repeat this three times to oxygenate and awaken your body. It's a great way to start the day.

In Nia, free dance is an important aspect of allowing the body to express feelings. Anyone can do it. All you have to do is put on some music, feel the emotions that the music elicits, and then allow your body to move in ways that naturally express these emotions. At the end of this chapter I have listed some of my favorite music to use.

Yoga

One of the reasons Yoga has become such an invaluable part of my wellness program is that it has helped me take control of a wandering mind and experience the feeling of being fully present and mind/body/spirit integrated. For me, doing some form of yoga is crucial for keeping me calm and centered and for giving me the energy I need to go about my day.

When I first tried to meditate I got so frustrated that I gave up quickly. It was only when I began to practice Yoga that I was able to begin to slow down my racing mind and focus.So if you have a chance to try a yoga class, please do. But be aware that finding a good Yoga teacher is like finding someone to cut your hair. It is very individual. So keep searching until you find a class that meets your needs. Just to help you along the way, let me describe some of the types of yoga you will encounter:

Hatha Yoga

Hatha Yoga is the umbrella term for the type of yoga that involves physical postures called asanas. Under the umbrella of Hatha Yoga are many different styles of teaching. Following are a few of the most common styles of teaching Hatha Yoga in the United States:

Iyengar Yoga: Focus on detailed instruction for correct alignment, technically demanding. Appeals to people who want a more intense workout.

Kripalu Yoga: Less detailed in mechanics and technique; more flowing, appeals to those who want a softer workout.

Integral Yoga: Traditional style which is more meditative. Appeals to people who want a more meditative experience.

Ashtanga Yoga: Often called "power yoga". Intense workout done with a heater and humidifier to warm muscles for deeper flexibility. Appeals to people who are well-conditioned and want an intense workout.

My advice in finding a yoga class is to try out several until you find one that meets your needs.

Some women are afraid to take a yoga class because they don't believe they are flexible enough. That's sort of like saying you don't want to go to the dentist to get your teeth cleaned because you are embarrassed by the poor condition of your teeth and gums. How else are they going to get better? Yoga isn't about physical perfection - it is about moving your body in and out of poses that are designed to heal the body and to connect mind, body and spirit.

Other women complain that they just can't stand yoga classes because they are so boring. To that I respond that the reason that yoga classes are boring is because we have become so addicted to complexity that we can't stand being still and focusing our mind on just one thing for more than 20 seconds. Our mind is liked a spoiled two-year-old. It doesn't want to sit still. And we let it do whatever it wants to do. Research in psychoneuroimmunology shows that every thought you have creates chemical shifts in your physiology. Negative thoughts and emotions like annoyance, irritation, anger, frustration, and impatience cause chemicals to be produced that are not healing. That is why it is so important to learn to control your own mind.

Yoga and Pregnancy

Yoga became such an important part of my life that when I was pregnant with my first child (at age 39), I decided to get certified in Prenatal Yoga so I could safely continue my yoga practice throughout my pregnancy. There is no doubt that if it weren't for the strength, flexibility and focus my yoga practice provided me, my labor and delivery would not have gone as well as it did. Thanks to my preparation and the loving care of a skilled midwife, I was able to have an unmedicated, vaginal delivery.

Fitness and Family/Work/Life

Once my baby arrived, however, my yoga practice took a nosedive, and I was not managing to eke out even 10 minutes of walking or riding the exercise bike. How in the world could I fit in exercise between nursing a baby every two hours? Even as he grew and I was able to space out the feedings, my new responsibilities overwhelmed me and I found myself getting anxious, fearful and resentful. Meanwhile, my physical body felt sluggish and tight. So I had to find a way to do my yoga and get some movement in the midst of feeding, changing and rocking a baby, taking care of other familial responsibilities AND continuing with my business.

Whether you have kids or not, work at home or not, are married or not, I hope my suggestions will help you to fit some movement into your day.

Making Strength and Flexibility a Part of Your Day

Movement is not just for physical benefits. Movement also affects the mind, emotions and spirit. Emotions such as fear, anger, and grief change the way we carry our bodies. If these emotions persist, we form a habit pattern. For example, when I'm nervous I find myself tightening my left buttock, lifting my left shoulder a bit, and leaning my head slightly forward. After a long evening of meeting new people I will often return home with a dagger pain above my left shoulder blade and in the left side of my lower back. For this reason, it is very important to release tension from your body every day.

The following stretches will help you de-stress your body. As you do them, focus on breathing to length-

38

en the spine on each inhale and relax into the stretch in each exhale. Work up to holding each stretch for 4 long breaths.

Chest Stretch (Fig. A)

Chest Stretch- to prevent rounding of the shoulders

Notice what happens to your chest whenever you feel embarrassed, ashamed, sad or afraid. It closes and tightens. To open the front of the chest, simply sit at the edge of your chair and grasp the back sides of the chair. Lift the center of your chest and breathe so deeply that it feels as though your chest is splitting open in the center. Stay for 4-6 breaths. See Fig. A.

Standing Hamstring Stretch (Fig. B)

Seated Hamstring Stretch (Fig. C)

Hamstring Stretch- to prevent lower back pain

The backs of your legs need to be stretched because if they stay tight it can contribute to low back pain. When you do this stretch use your imagination and pretend that as you inhale the breath goes to the tightest spot and spreads open the muscle fibers. Then as you exhale, imagine that the muscles release from the bone. If you are standing to do this stretch, place your hand on a table or counter top. Then walk your feet back until your back is flat like a tabletop and your feet are directly under your hips. Keep your arms by your ears. See Fig. B.

If you are sitting, simply extend one leg in front of you. Inhale and lengthen your spine, and as you exhale, bend forward from the hip socket (not from the waist). Stay for 4 or 6 breaths. See Fig. C.

Half Spinal Twist - to release tension along the spine

This is one of my favorite stretches. When I work at the computer for long hours, I find myself spontaneously doing a half spinal twist to release tension all along the spine. To perform the stretch, sit at the edge of your chair. Place your feet directly under your knees and put your knees together. Turn to your left and use your left hand to hold on toward the back of the seat. Place your right hand on the left side of the left knee. Inhale to lengthen the spine. As you exhale, gently press the right hand against the left knee and pull with the left hand to twist your spine. Be sure to keep the knees facing forward. Hold the stretch for 4 - 6 breaths and then slowly release the hands and return to the forward-facing position. Repeat on the other side. See Fig. D.

Hip Stretch- to prevent sciatic nerve pain

Our hips get extremely tight during the course of the day, especially if we continuously sit at a desk or in a car a lot or carry a baby on one hip. This stretch is particularly useful in preventing sciatic pain (if you don't know what sciatic pain is, be thankful - and do this stretch so you may never know this shooting pain from your low back down the back of your leg!) You can sit in a chair or stand holding a bar or the counter edge. Cross one ankle over the opposite knee and press down the knee. As you inhale, lengthen your sternum (breastbone) away from your pubic bone. Then as you exhale, hinge from the hip socket and bend forward. Stay for 4 to 6 breaths. See Fig. E.

Half Spinal Twist (Fig. D)

Hip Stretch (Fig. E)

Groin Stretch

The groin and inner thighs rarely get stretched in the normal course of the day - unless you change some of your normal activities. Whenever I sit down to write a letter, read a book or magazine or play with the baby, I always spend a few minutes sitting in a straddle position on the floor. In fact, I wrote most of this book using my laptop computer, sitting on the floor in a straddle position. See Fig. F.

Groin Stretch (Fig. F)

Calf Stretch

Even if you never wore high heels, chances are good that your calf muscles are tight. There are many ways to stretch this muscle, but my favorite is using stairs. Just be careful not to over-do it. Start out by letting the heel only sink a little lower than the step, while keeping your other foot on the same step for balance. Then, if you feel like it, you can lift the other foot off the step to intensify the stretch.

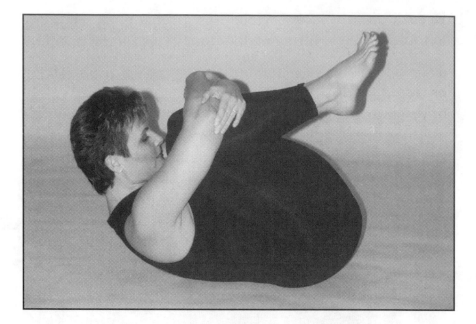

Low Back Stretch (Fig. G)

Low Back Stretch

Probably the most common complaint is low back pain. The above stretches will help keep your low back comfortable, but this stretch is specifically for the low back. The perfect time to do it is in bed, when you first awaken in the morning and just before you go to sleep at night. Hug your knees into your chest and wrap your arms around them as tightly as possible. Bring your forehead as close to your knees as you can and take a deep breath. Feel how the breath expands your lower back. Now, take in a little more air. Then let it all out with a sigh. See Fig. G.

Breath of Joy- to energize you

To help wake you up, get out of bed and take three deep breaths while standing. This is my favorite wake up breath! To do it, inhale fully through the nose as you bring the arms overhead, and then exhale forcefully through the mouth as you quickly press the arms down and bend the knees. Repeat 4 - 6 times. See Fig. H and I.

Breath of Joy - Part 1 (Fig. H)

Breath of Joy - Part 2 (Fig. I)

Triceps dips- to prevent sagging arm muscles

Through personal experience, I have found that unless your triceps muscle is used, the backs of your arms will flop and jiggle when you wave or write on a chalk-board. Here is a simple way to work those muscles at home.

To perform this exercise, sit at the edge of a chair. Make sure that the chair has a firm seat. If it is too soft, your wrists will hyperextend. Keeping your wrist straight, bend the elbows and lower your body. Then straighten the elbows to lift your body upwards. Be sure to keep the neck long and prevent sinking into the shoulders. Repeat 8 - 15 times. See Fig. J.

Triceps Dip (Fig. J)

Push-Ups

One of the most effective exercises for arms and upper body is the push-up. A great way to do push-ups during the day is to use tables or counter tops. Place your hands wide enough that your hands are directly under your elbows when they are bent. As you lower your body, imagine that you are attempting to touch your chest to the edge of the table, not your nose. Keep your neck in alignment with your spine. See Fig. K.

Push-Ups (Fig. K)

Pelvic Floor Muscles

Every woman can benefit from strengthening the pelvic floor muscles. Women who have strong pelvic muscles (pubococcygeous or PC muscles) are less prone to vaginal problems and urinary stress incontinence. They also tend to have more fulfilling sexual experiences. Often called Kegel exercises (named after Dr. Kegel), pelvic floor exercises have been practiced for thousands of years in ancient Taoist practices and Tantric Yoga practices. They are especially important for women during pregnancy and birth.

How do you work these muscles? Try this: to get a sense of how you can contract and release your pelvic floor muscles, stop the flow of urine midstream. This is not something you should do often- it is just to give you an idea of which muscles you are looking for. Another way to find the pelvic floor muscles is to insert one finger into your vagina and contract your vaginal muscles around your finger. These are also the muscles which grip the penis when making love.

How to perform Kegel exercises:

1. Close your eyes and focus your awareness on your pelvic floor.
2. Tighten your pelvic floor muscles by drawing them up toward your uterus. Just your pelvic floor muscles should be moving, not your buttocks or abdominal muscles.
3. Breathe out and let them release slowly.
4. Continue, inhaling as you tighten and exhaling as you release. Repeat four times.
5. Once you can do this, tighten the pelvic floor muscles when you inhale, and hold them tight for fives seconds. Breathe normally, then release them slowly.

Discipline

I know it sounds like a very dirty word. But discipline is what you need when you've been accustomed to not moving your body, because you can't remember how good you can really feel. So at the very beginning it will take some discipline to just get started. This means that if you decide you can walk for 15 minutes on your lunch break or that you can go up and down the stairs in your house 10 extra times in one day, then you HAVE TO DO IT.

How do you begin to discipline yourself when your schedule is not your own - when you are constantly having to change your plans based on the needs of others? Make a flexible schedule - but not so flexible that it stretches into the next day. You'll be amazed how many movement activities you can fit into your day when you have a clear focus and intention to do so. Here is a sample flexible schedule along with the actual events that occurred using it:

Sample Flexible Schedule

In bed: back stretches
Just out of bed: breathe
While fixing breakfast: hamstring stretch at the kitchen
        counter
Playing with baby: straddle stretch, triceps presses
Using stairs: 5 extra trips up and down, calf stretch
Middle of the afternoon: hip stretch and hamstring
        stretch in your chair
After dinner: walk with anyone in the family who wants
        to come, or dance in your living room.

For the woman who goes to an office everyday, the schedule is really not that much different. Use the stretches that can be done in a chair while sitting at your desk. It might even help you to have a printed schedule posted where you can see it. I actually found it easier to create a more fixed schedule when I worked in an office outside of my home than when I worked in my home.

Here is a sample schedule from my office days:

In bed: back stretches

Just out of bed: breathing exercises

In car: Kegels at every red light

Mid morning: walk 5 flights of stairs to restroom (even though there was one on my floor- this was an easy way to get a little invigorating activity without anyone noticing I was gone for too long). This one is tricky. If you really NEED to go, go to the restroom on your floor first, then walk the stairs. Also, make sure to do a calf stretch at the end of the stair adventure.

11:00 am: hip stretch and hamstring and chest stretch in chair

Lunch: walk for 20 minutes after eating

Mid afternoon: 5 flights of stairs to the restroom again. If I had the restroom to myself I would do breathing exercises to revitalize me and prevent me from craving a candy bar and soda.

Cooking Dinner: push ups at counter and triceps dips

In bed: low back stretches

How to Create Your Own Schedule

The best way to create your own schedule is to decide what exercises you feel will benefit you. Then split them up into two days so that you aren't trying to do them all each day. Try to imagine where you could sneak in the activities within the context of your day's activities and then write it down. It takes a while to remember to slide in these activities - but don't give up. Before you know it, you will find yourself doing push-ups on the side of your car while waiting for your car to fill with gas or subtly doing calf stretches off the side of the curb while waiting for the morning bus. The best part is that you haven't had to take away from any of the activities and responsibilities that you already were doing.

Aerobic Activities for Tight Schedules

I found that turning on some of my favorite music and dancing worked great when the baby was taking a nap or sitting in his swing. Sometimes it would only last for 5 or 10 minutes, but the calorie-burning, oxygen-pumping experience would lift my mood and give me more energy. The important thing is that I had to keep my commitment to myself to dance at least once a day - even for only a few minutes.

Without a doubt, walking is one of the best overall cardiovascular exercises. If you could walk briskly for 45 minutes a day, your physical body would change dramatically and your energy level would be boosted. Two walks of 20 or 25 minutes are just as good as one long walk, so don't feel that you must find a 45-minute block of time. When you walk, keep your elbows bent at a 90-degree angle and use your arm swing to help power your walk. This will improve your posture and strengthen your arms, making your walk a full-body toning activity, as well as an aerobic activity.

I've only listed a few of the exercises that you could be doing for strength and flexibility. If you want to learn more, the following list of books will provide plenty!

Resources:

Yogiraj Sri Swami Satchidananda. (1970) <u>Integral Yoga Hatha</u>. Henry Holt and Company.

Birch, Beryl Bender. (1995) <u>Power Yoga.</u> Fireside

Jordan, Sandra. (1987) <u>Yoga for Pregnancy.</u> St. Martin's Press.

Andes, Karen (1995) <u>A Woman's Book of Strength.</u> The Berkley Publishing Group.

Andes, Karen (1998) <u>A Woman's Book of Power</u>. The Berkley Publishing Group

Walker, Peter and Fiona (1987) <u>Natural Parenting</u>. Gaia Books, Ltd.

Lusk, Julie (1998) <u>Desktop Yoga</u>. Perigree.

Mahta, Silva, Mira & Shyam. (1990) <u>Yoga the Iyengar Way</u>. Alfred A. Knopf

Lasater, Judith. (1995) <u>Relax and Renew</u>. Rodmell Press

Rosas, Debbie and Rosas, Carlos. (1987) <u>NIA- Non Impact Aerobics</u>. (order by calling 1-800-762-5762)

To find Nia teachers in your area, purchase Nia videos or inquire about becoming a certified Nia teacher call 1-800-762-5762

Suggested Music:

Music you can't find at the store- but you must have!:
Songs for the Inner Child, by Shaina Noll
Call: 1-800-852-3821 or visit the website at
WWW.cybervillage.com/Starburst

Brave Faith, by Jana Stanfield
Call: 1-888-530-5262 or visit the website at
WWW.songs.com/Jana

Here are a few of my favorite CD's for dancing around in
the living room and doing Nia:

Walela by Rita Coolidge
Shaman's Breath by Professor Trance and the Energisers
Music Box and Butterfly by Mariah Carey
The French Album by Celine Dion
Older by George Michael
Leap of Faith and The Unimaginable Life by Kenny Loggins
One World and Latino, Latino by Putumayo World Music
The Meeting Pool by Baka Beyond
Don't Ask by Tina Arena
Wakafrica by Manu Dibango
The Mask and the Mirror by Loreena McKennitt
Divas Live by VH1 Music First
Gloria by Gloria Estefan
Aye by Angelique Kidjo
Big Bad Voodoo Daddy by Big Bad Voodoo Daddy

Chapter IV
Nourishment: How to Feed
Hungry Bodies and Minds

One of the questions I am frequently asked by women is, "How can I get rid of _____?" The blank is usually filled with specific body parts or simply the word "fat." Why is it so many women want to lose weight and get rid of hips, thighs and tummies? I believe the reason is multifaceted.

The biggest reason is the societal definition of what a woman should look like. According to current societal norms, we should have the flat abdomen of an adolescent boy, size 36C, perky breasts, and absolutely no visible body fat on our hips, thighs or buttocks. This body may be possible for a few of us during a few years of our lives (like between 16 and 22 years of age), but as we experience life, have children and shift hormonally, this false picture of a "healthy woman" is, in reality, the picture of a woman obsessed with diet, exercise and plastic surgery. This means that women who do not even need to lose weight are still obsessed with losing weight.

Food and body image are so connected for women that I cannot write about one without the other. Body image is so crucial to a woman's overall health that, to give it justice, I have dedicated a separate chapter to the subject.

The obsession with thinness explains the thriving, 36 billion-dollar diet industry in our country. It's insane! If you go to any book store and look in the health and fitness section you will find hundreds of titles relating to diet - many of which directly oppose each other in theory and practice. Should you eat many small meals throughout the day, or should you eat three meals and nothing after 8 p.m.? Should you eat only fruit before noon, only protein at noon and a shake for dinner or should you eat a shake for breakfast and lunch and have a high protein dinner? Should you eat more carbohydrates and less fat or more protein and less carbohydrate? There seems to be no end to this insanity!

I call the current diet mentality "dietary schizophrenia". The diet industry loves the confusion because it guarantees that you will continue to buy books and products in your search for the answer.... when the answer lies inside of you, and it has been there all along. It's sort of like Dorothy in the Wizard of Oz when Glenda, the Good Witch, tells her she's always had the power to go home. You, too, have the power to know how much, how often and what type of food will nourish your body, mind and soul. If only you would just take time to listen and trust yourself. The problem is that we have forgotten how to trust ourselves.

"Today many businesses offering to help you reduce your body size are just a racket. Weight-reduction books, weight-reduction recipes, weight-reduction corporations! It's real nonsense. What's the harm in having a few extra pounds? As long as you don't fall sick, it's all right to be a little heavier than the average. If you feel

healthy, you don't need to reduce to become slim like someone else. We are not all built the same way. Why should we look the same? We should just accept what and who we are. We don't have to imitate others. Remember a deer is a deer, and an elephant is an elephant. Some vegetables are slim like string beans. Others are plump as pumpkins. Both are vegetables. Should the pumpkin want to imitate the string bean? Be who you are and don't worry constantly when you eat or drink."
Sri Swami Satchidananda

Many people are carrying extra pounds that make us feel lethargic. For us, it's not just that we want to look like a fashion model, we just want our energy back. One reason many of us put on extra pounds is because of poor lifestyle choices. If you look at the incidence of obesity in the early 1900's you'll find that it was somewhere around 4 percent—a far cry from the 40 percent estimated today. It makes sense when you look at the lifestyle at the turn of the century. Physical activity was built into every day. For instance, you may remember from Chapter 1 what Monday was a hundred years ago: wash DAY. When is the last time you spent an entire day doing wash? That doesn't mean just dropping the wash in and letting it run while you do other things. That means actually scrubbing the clothes, wringing them out, hanging them in the sun, taking them off the line and then folding them!

Even cooking dinner was physically demanding. The average meal took 5 1/2 hours to prepare: you had to chase the chicken, wring its neck, pluck its feathers, gather wood, stoke the fire, carry water, pick the vegetables, knead the dough, and churn the butter. No wonder the average 120-pound woman could eat more than 2,400 calories a day and maintain her weight. Now the average sedentary 120-pound woman can only eat around 1,400 calories and maintain her weight.

"The labor of the human body is rapidly being engineered out of working life."
John F. Kennedy

In order to maintain a healthy weight, we are not only limited to fewer calories than our sisters of 100 years ago, but we often must have smaller portions because we choose foods higher in fat than they did. In 1900, the average diet was around 60% carbohydrate, 10% protein and 30% fat. That's because animal products were harder to obtain and store than agricultural products. Interestingly, the 1900 diet resembles the diet currently suggested by the American Dietetic Association for good health. The average diet of today, however, is much higher in fat and protein. And since one ounce of fat contains more than twice as many calories as one ounce of carbohydrate or protein, it means that today's woman not only must eat fewer calories because of her relative lack of physical activity- she must also eat very small portions if she continues to eat foods high in fat.

No wonder we have a problem!

Food and Mood

To top off the lack of physical activity and the increase in fat consumption, we also have to deal with cravings! Sarah Leibowitz, Ph.D., a professor of neuro-biology at Rockefeller University, has pioneered research on the body's control center for food cravings. Interestingly, the body's cravings center is next door to the reproduction center in our brain. Dr. Leibowitz speculates that this may be no coincidence. The body's fundamental drive to survive and reproduce must ensure that it receive enough food to not only meet current energy demands, but also prepare for potential famine.

When I was visiting Lake Austin Spa Resort one of the most popular lectures was called "Food and Mood". Resident dietician Terry Shaw, MS, LD, had a great way of explaining cravings. Some cravings are biochemically driven: the brain releases neuropeptides that actually create cravings. For instance, Neuropeptide Y (NPY) is released in the morning and it triggers a desire for carbo-hydrates. It's as if the brain whispers to you "eat some carbohydrates, please." If you ignore the whisper, then by lunch the voice is a bit louder and it says, "eat some carbohydrates." If you continue to ignore the voice, then by 3:00 p.m. it says, "EAT SOME CARBOHY-DRATES!" which, unfortunately, usually leads to a candy bar or bag of chips instead of a baked potato or a bowl of cereal. If for some reason you ignore the voice until the end of the day you are very likely to find your-self cleaning out the pantry as the voice screams relent-lessly, "EAT CARBOHYDRATES NOW!"

Galanin is another neuropeptide released by the brain. It is released when you haven't eaten for a while (when your body begins to break down its own body fat for energy). And it says, "Eat some fat." If you don't heed its wishes, you will end up the same way you did when you didn't heed the voice of NPY - bingeing on fat-laden food.

Galanin levels start out low in the morning and rise throughout the day. They also rise when estrogen levels are high, which might explain the cravings for sweet-and-creamy foods associated with PMS.

Fad diets, which generate a flood of metabolic debris, also increase galanin levels, which ultimately triggers a fat craving. Interestingly, stress hormones such as norepinephrine and corticosterone raise galanin levels, too. That explains why many of us start stalking the refrigerator or pantry when we are feeling stressed, which includes anything from boredom to anxiety.

The bottom line is: listen to your body. If it says eat some fat, then eat some fat. If it says eat some carbohydrate, then eat some carbohydrate. But, as Terry would say, "eat a slice of bread, not the whole loaf!"

Biological causes for cravings are only part of the picture. Another component of cravings is an emotional phenomenon called "entrainment". Entrainment occurs when you have an experience while eating a certain food and then mentally and emotionally link the experience with the food. When I was growing up, my dad always made potato soup for lunch after church on Sundays. This was a very special time for our family because my dad, being a young physician at the time, was rarely present for meals during the week. So this was a time that we could all be together - and I remember feeling safe, warm and secure. Well, my freshman year at Vanderbilt Nursing School I was very, very homesick. I'll never forget one Sunday walking toward the cafeteria for lunch: as I approached I could smell the potato soup being served that day and I immediately burst into tears as homesickness washed over me. I spent the next hour on a long-distance phone call with my parents.

Food entrainment also creates aversions. The classic example is the situation of a young child who vomitted just after eating something. For my ten-year-old stepson it was spaghetti with tomato sauce. He loves plain spaghetti and he loves tomato sauce on pizza, but there is no way you can get him to eat spaghetti with tomato sauce! I'm sure you've had such an aversion to food in your life.

Many women ask me, "how can we create aversions to chocolate and pastries?" The best answer I have for that question is that you must create new memories. For instance, if you pay attention to the way you feel when you eat high fat, high sugar foods, you may begin to notice that you don't really feel well. So perhaps you could begin to recall that new feeling when you are considering eating those foods. However, the bottom line still remains, "listen to your body - but just because you are craving chocolate doesn't mean you have to eat the whole box!"

Speaking of chocolate, if you are one of the millions of women who crave chocolate from time to time, you might be interested in the following chocolate facts from Debra Waterhouse's book, Why Women Need Chocolate:

* 97 percent of all women surveyed report food cravings, 68 percent of which are for chocolate

* 50 percent of all women surveyed say they would
    choose chocolate over sex
* women are 22 times more likely than men to choose
    chocolate as a mood enhancer
* 3.4 million dollars are spent annually on chocolate, the
    majority of it comes from women's wallets

Why is chocolate such a craved food? The psychological, or entrainment, reasons are obvious: it was given to you as a reward since childhood and it has been used as a romantic gift since you began dating. But you may not have been aware of the biological reasons for the craving:

1) it contains phenylethylamine, the same chemical
    released in our brain when we fall in love
2) it contains theobromine, a substance similar to caffeine
    that stimulates us
3) it contains sugar, which in turn increases the release of
    serotonin, the hormone that makes us feel calm and
    relaxed
4) it contains fat, which also increases the release of
    endorphins, the hormone that lifts your spirits
5) it contains magnesium, a mineral involved in
    manufacturing serotonin and stabilizing mood

You see, your body is very, very wise - even when it is craving chocolate. The good news is that it only takes one or two Hershey Kisses to satisfy a biological craving for chocolate. At 25 calories a piece, this will not undo a healthy eating plan. However, what will undo a healthy eating plan is to restrict chocolate, for as long as you can stand it, and then binge on the whole bag of Kisses.

When you begin to understand the connection between neuropeptides, memories, emotions and cravings you also begin to understand why most diets fail. Most diets are based on restrictive eating. You can do well for a while, but if the diet is not providing you with adequate nutrition, chemicals will be produced that will make you crave certain foods. Or even if the diet is nutritionally sound, you may go into a situation or an environment that has such a strong entrainment with a certain food that you literally feel powerless over the food. For instance, even after eating a hearty and satisfying Thanksgiving meal, many people can't resist a piece of Grandma's Pumpkin Pie because it brings back so many wonderful memories. How about walking into a movie theater- your mouth waters with the desire for popcorn!

Trusting Cravings

How do you know whether to trust your cravings or not? First, go back to the chapter on body types and ask yourself the six questions at the end of the chapter. Although I agree with the leading experts in the field of non-restrictive eating, who suggest that you eat according to your cravings, I also know that when a person is out of balance she usually craves the very foods that will push her more and more out of balance. Typically, when Air is out of balance you forget to eat and skip meals. When Fire is out of balance you crave salty, spicy and/or fried foods and alcohol. When Earth is out of balance you crave sweet and/or creamy foods. If you notice that you are out of balance and are craving these foods then you must find a way to bring yourself back into balance first, and then you can trust your instincts.

Which program should I follow?

I think it's valuable to learn more about time-tested nutritional programs such as Ayurvedic or macrobiotic. In fact, when I was recovering from having my baby I followed a specific food and herb program recommended by an Ayurvedic physician - and it helped me tremendously. If you do decide to learn about one of these systems of healing through food, I recommend that you stick with the same system for at least three months before you switch and try another.

Each person will find a unique solution. Here are some of the ways my clients and I have successfully dealt with cravings and have discovered what style of eating helps us feel our best:

1. Instead of eating 3 large meals, experiment with having snacks in mid-morning, mid-afternoon and evening. They don't have to be big snacks, but something with protein and carbohydrate to keep galanin and NPY from being released.

2. Experiment by slowly decreasing fat intake. For instance, while I was pregnant I got into the habit of eating a bowl of homemade vanilla ice cream every night. After the baby was born I still had that craving every night. But since I was 25 pounds heavier than my pre-pregnancy weight, I wanted to find a way to curb that craving. I started by substituting a low-fat version of ice cream. Then I began to have vanilla yogurt (the kind in a cup, not frozen). Then I substituted with a banana, and finally with an apple. Now I occasionally have a bowl of ice cream, but the craving has truly subsided! It is impor-

tant to note that it does take at least 21 days to create a new habit. So for the first few weeks you will have to exercise a good amount of discipline on this one.

3. Increase your intake of fresh fruits and vegetables. The soluble fibers in these foods are especially effective in curbing erratic swings in blood-sugar levels, which ultimately helps reduce food cravings.

4. Plan ahead. Good nutrition does not happen by itself! I know, because I remember times that when I got off work, I was starving. I would eat anything in sight, whether I really liked it or not! I got in the habit of carrying a plastic container of air-popped popcorn in my car (this is the only food that can withstand the heat in an enclosed car during a Texas summer). Now that I am at home with a baby I pop the popcorn while I'm mixing his cereal in the morning. I keep it on the kitchen counter in that same plastic container so that it is ready whenever I need a quick snack.

5. Avoid situations that predispose you for cravings. For instance, if I pass by the ice cream parlor on my way home, I am much more likely to succumb to a fleeting craving for homemade vanilla than I am if I take another road. Also, if I go inside to pay for my gas, rather than paying at the pump, I am much more likely to crave a candy bar - just as someone with a dominant Fire nature might find themselves buying chips, beef jerky or peanuts.

6. Experiment with eating warm, moist foods; warm, dry foods; cold, moist foods; and cold dry foods. Keep a log

like the one at the end of this chapter to see which type of food helps you feel better and prevent cravings.

7.   Create different feelings by planning what you eat accordingly. Rather than waiting for feelings to occur, you can actually create feelings you desire by choosing the right foods for you. Most of us desire feelings like calm and peace, joy and happiness, or focus and purpose. It turns out that those feelings are caused by the release of certain neurotransmitters - and different foods can cause the release of these neurotransmitters.

By choosing carbohydrates, proteins or fats, you can proactively affect your mood state.
Eat carbohydrates to feel relaxed and calm
The neurotransmitter serotonin creates feelings of calmness and peace. When you eat carbohydrates you stimulate the release of serotonin and the following cascade of events is likely:
* feeling of relaxation and calmness
* decreased depression
* decreased pain sensitivity
* decreased food intake
* promotion of muscle growth
* promotion of heat production (wastes calories)
It is interesting to note that mood-elevating drugs such as Prozac function by allowing serotonin to linger longer at the receiving nerve cell, thus increasing the length and strength of the stimulation to that nerve cell.

Eat fat to feel joyous and happy temporarily. For longer-lasting effects, exercise, laugh or get romantic!

The neurotransmitter endorphin is often called the body's natural opiate. It creates the feelings of euphoria, joy, and happiness. Eating fat stimulates the release of endorphins, but unfortunately eating fat provides a short-term effect. That is why people tend to go back for more. Exercise also promotes the release of endorphins, but its effect is long term. Endorphin levels after exercise will be higher for as long as 12 - 24 hours! Other activities that promote the release of endorphins are laughter, recalling very happy memories, romance, immersion in water, and orgasm.

The release of endorphins causes:
* euphoria and mood stability
* increased fat mobilization
* decreased depression

So if laughing or recalling happy memories can stimulate the release of endorphins, then you could say that to feel joyous and happy, all you have to do is be joyous and happy!

Eat protein to focus and concentrate

The neurotransmitter, dopamine, creates the feeling of mental focus and concentration. When you eat even small amounts of protein, this neurotransmitter is released.

It causes:
* increased vigor
* increased energy
* increased concentration and focus

But I still want to know what I should be eating...

The truth about diet is that it is very individual. For every diet book on the shelf there is someone who felt good following the plan and a hundred others who felt terrible. To know what works best for you, pay attention to how you feel when you eat certain foods. The best way to do this is to take an inventory of your current eating patterns. I know this is probably as appealing to you as balancing your checkbook, but it's just as important. Many of us don't have a clue what or when we are eating on a daily basis. The inventory on the following page will help you begin to see when you are typically hungry, what food you crave, what emotions drive you, and how you feel. I suggest that you make several copies of it and keep an inventory for at least one month.

Time of Day	Food Item Eaten	Food Item Desired	How you felt prior to eating	How you felt after eating

Fasting

Sometimes it helps to take a sabbatical from eating, so when you start eating again, you can really sense how certain foods make you feel.

" The minute we stop eating, the body starts housecleaning. Fasting is one of nature's oldest tools."
Nutritionist, Daya Oliver

Although fasting is not for everyone (especially not for women with dominant Air nature), many nutrition experts believe that periodically giving your digestive system a rest can do wonders in eliminating waste and toxins from the body. Linda Villarosa, in her book Body & Soul, points out that fasting or giving up particular foods has been used for centuries among Yoruba religious traditions, Muslim Ramadan and Christian Lent. Eastern religions and philosophies also include fasting for purification, heightened spirituality and healing. Some people are able to fast on diluted apple juice for a day, add in plain vegetables and fruits the next day, include lean proteins the next, then complex carbohydrates, and finally fats. You could create your own "spa week" where you followed a plan like this for a week in order to "clean your palate". It will help you become more aware of how food affects you. You will also notice after a period of fasting or eating simple fruits, vegetables and lean protein that you enjoy your food much more. But one of the best things is that you are more easily satisfied.

If you are willing to try adventurous vegetarian fare, and would like to read more about using a short fast to help you tune into your body's signals, you would enjoy Feeling Light by Judith Katzman and Wendy Shankin-Cohen. In their book they outline a way to discover which foods restore you body's internal balance. I really like their approach. But you must be willing to take some time to read, and you will have to shop in some specialty food stores.

If you just don't have time to read anything new or shop in any new stores, and you don't really like to cook, then you can do what I do. Once you know which foods give you the energy you desire, plan your menu each week on Saturday or Sunday making a list of the foods you need in order to have snacks and meals that satisfy you. Once you have the list, go to the grocery store around 8:00 p.m. while it is fairly empty and buy everything you'll need for the week. Post the menus on the refrigerator so nobody eats the food you'll need for tomorrow's dinner. Each morning, take out the vegetables and fruits that will be eaten that day. This helps ensure that they actually get eaten and don't go bad in your refrigerator!

I dislike cooking so much that I only make seven dinners, and I rotate them each week. They change a bit based on which vegetables or fruits I serve, but I only have seven main meals.

Your Inner Voice

Having counseled hundreds of women and dealt with food issues myself, I believe that the most important place to look for information is inside of you. If you have trouble hearing your inner voice, I would suggest that you experiment with some of the suggestions in this book such as practicing yoga and meditation. Also, you might want to read one of the following books. They will encourage you to listen to your inner voice when making food choices. Each author has a different approach to helping you find that voice, just as each of you has a unique voice.

Resources

Debra Waterhouse (1995) Why Women Need Chocolate. Hyperion.

Jane Hirschman and Carol Munter (1998) Overcoming Overeating. Fawcett Books.

Andrew Weil, 8 Weeks to Optimal Health (1997) Alfred A. Knopf.

Elizabeth Somer (1995) Food and Mood. Henry Holt.

Ann Louise Gittleman (1996) Your Body Knows Best. Pocket Books.

Christiane Northrup (1994) Women's Bodies, Women's Wisdom. Bantam Books.

Chapter V
Your Body Knows
What You're Thinking

"A heart at peace gives life to the body, but envy rots the bones." Proverbs 14:30

"A cheerful look brings joy to the heart, and good news gives health to the bones." Proverbs 15:30

"Pleasant words are a honeycomb, sweet to the soul and healing to the bones." Proberbs 16:34

"A cheerful heart is good medicine, but a crushed spirit dries up the bones." Proverbs 17:22

Since the 1950s there has been an increased interest in how our mental and emotional states affect our health, either helping to keep us well or making us more susceptible to illness. In fact, studies have shown that over 50 percent of all patients seen by general practice physicians do not have organic illnesses. In other words, there are not physical causes that can be treated by conventional medical techniques. As you read in Chapter 1, we now know that our minds and our immune systems work closely together.

You also know from personal experience that your state of mind has a lot to do with how good you feel. In other words, you feel the way you think. Here's an example:

One of my favorite summer activities is to hang glide in Nagshead, North Carolina. If you were to go with me, we would strap into harnesses suspended from the kite, pick up the aluminum bar that steers the glider, run off the edge of the cliff and soar like a bird. Moving our bodies left and right we could steer the glider, and when it was time to land we would gently press the bar away from us and land on our feet. Some of you would be feeling exhilarated and full of energy - ready to go again. But others of you would be feeling sick at your stomach, nervous and jittery.

The interesting thing is that we all had the same experience. We all strapped into our gliders, ran off the cliff, flew down and landed safely. So it wasn't the experience that caused us to feel either exhilarated or ill, it was our perception of the experience.

Present Time

When I find my mind spinning out of control, worrying about a potential future disaster or fretting over a past incident, I bring myself into present time. The breathing practices in Chapter 7 and the meditation practices in Chapter 9 will be helpful to you in doing this. Here is the process I use:

1. Take three deep breaths.
2. Pay attention to present time events such as your heart beating inside of your chest, your breathing, or the warmth of the sun on your skin.
3. Say to yourself something like this: "Right now I am not in any danger, I am not too hot or too cold, I am not hungry, I am not in pain..."

This exercise takes only a couple of minutes to do, and it often stops the "spin cycle" in my mind.

"People will be just about as happy as they will allow themselves to be."
Abraham Lincoln

Distorted Thoughts

Sometimes the thoughts that are spinning in my mind are stronger than I am, and I can't even bring myself into present time. The thoughts scream at me of disaster, doom, defeat, should's and ought's. The voice becomes so loud that I can't quiet my mind long enough to even take a deep breath. In this case I have found it helpful to do a little "surgery" on my thoughts - to cut them out and analyze them.

Let me use myself as an example to illustrate the concept of distorted thinking. Ever since I left a structured, corporate job, my shortcomings in the area of organization became very apparent; therefore, I have had to work on improving my organizational skills. This year I alphabetized my library, color-coded my files, computerized my invoicing and banking system and began to keep a mailing list database. However, in one particularly busy month, I got behind. In my rush to put together my presentation materials, pack my bags and prepare meals for my family, I let things slide. I left my library in a mess and I didn't balance my checkbook, record invoices, answer voice mails, return correspondence or pay bills. Upon my return from four trips that month, I saw the mess and had the following thoughts:

I knew I couldn't keep up this organization! I am such a slob! Now I'm never going to be able to catch up. I probably have overdrawn my checking account. I should never have left town without balancing the checkbook first. I don't know why I ever thought I could make a living like this. I'm no good at managing my own business. I'm going to have to quit speaking and take a "real" job.

If I had let my thoughts continue like this I would have been flung into a state of anxiety and fear about my financial stability. Then, paralyzed by fear, I would not have been able to motivate myself to organize the mess I had left. I would have spiraled into depression and hopelessness. Fortunately, I am aware of how illogical my thoughts can be so I was able to "surgically remove" and analyze them.

The biggest help in analyzing these thoughts came to me in Dr. David Burns' book, <u>Feeling Good: The New Mood Therapy</u>. In it he lists ten common cognitive distortions. Cognitive distortions are like looking at the world through a pair of eyeglasses that are the wrong prescription, or like looking into the trick mirrors at the fair that make you look too fat, skinny, short or tall. Here are some of the distortions in my thoughts from the previous example.

1. All-or-Nothing Thinking: By looking at things in absolute, black-and-white categories, I thought that just because I had let my organization slide I was now completely disorganized.

2. Overgeneralization: I viewed one episode of poor organization and business management as a never-ending pattern of defeat.

78

3. Mental Filter: By dwelling on this negative event I let it discolor my entire view of life. Rather than enjoying the successes of four keynote addresses, I focused on the impending failure of my business due to my poor management skills.

4. Discounting the Positives: I ignored the fact that I had made many positive organizational changes until that point.

5. Jumping to Conclusions: I concluded that everything with my business would fail because of my lack of organization. (This is also called fortune-telling.)

6. Emotional Reasoning: Just because I felt like a poor business manager at the moment, I reasoned that I must be one.

7. "Should" Statements: I criticized myself for something I "should" have done. As one of my good friends, always says, "stop 'shoulding' on yourself!"

8. Magnification: I blew things out of proportion.

9. Labeling: Instead of saying, "I let things slide last month." I labeled myself "a slob".

10. Blame: I blamed myself for something that had many contributing factors. For instance, I might have been able to complete the business management and organization if I had not prepared the presentation materials for my speeches - but that would not have been a wise decision.

Once you are able to recognize the distortions in your thinking you will be able to see the situation more realistically. In my case I was able to see that, given the situation, I had done the best I could do. And although I felt like a slob - it was only a feeling, not necessarily a permanent characteristic. I reminded myself of all the positive changes I had made throughout the year, and I affirmed to myself that I was getting more organized each day. Because I did not allow myself to wallow in despair or spin out of control in anxiety, I was able to chip away at organizing files, balancing checkbooks, returning correspondence and updating my invoices, while continuing to grow my business.

The Art of Letting Go

Sometimes, even when we recognize that our thoughts are distorted and illogical we still can't let them go. When I was training to become a Hatha Yoga teacher, Swami Satchidananda told us this parable: Long ago in India, hunters had a very clever way of capturing monkeys. They hollowed out a gourd, cut a hole in it just large enough to put a banana inside and then attached the gourd to a tree. When a monkey came along he would notice the banana inside of the gourd and reach his hand in to get it. As soon as the monkey grabbed the banana, he was trapped because the hole was too small for his clenched fist. If the monkey would have only let go of the banana he could have freed himself. Poor monkey...he sealed his own fate because his mind couldn't give up the idea of grabbing the fruit. Even when he saw the approaching hunters he wouldn't let go of the banana to free himself. He was literally a prisoner of his own mind!

Like the monkey, most of us have thoughts that we know are disturbing our peace of mind, but we just can't let them go. When I was a personal trainer in Washington, DC, I had a client who couldn't let go of the anger associated with her divorce. Every Saturday morning we would begin our session with a brisk three-mile walk, and invariably the subject of her divorce would surface. When she talked about it, her jaws and fists would clench and her breath would shorten. She was so disturbed by her divorce that she blamed her inability to enjoy life on it. Imagine my surprise, when during our third session I asked her how long ago she had divorced her husband and she responded, "twelve years ago." I couldn't believe it. For twelve years she had held on to the feelings of abandonment, isolation, fear, anger, loss and grief. She was unable to open her heart and mind, and let them go. Just like the monkey, she was a prisoner of her own mind.

Letting go is simple, but not easy. For me, the practice of meditation has been a wonderful teacher in the art of letting go. I recommend to all of my clients that they begin this practice immediately. It takes lots of practice to actually be able to let go of the patterns which create disturbing thoughts. If you don't already have an active meditation practice, be sure to read the chapter on meditation in this book. Start practicing today.

The Need to be Right

The need to be right is a trick of the mind that is guaranteed to disturb your peace. When you hang on to the need to be right, it is the same mistake as dwelling on negative thoughts. It is a trap that not only destroys your peace of mind, but can also destroy your relationships.

I seem to avoid this trap in every area of my life except in my relationship with my husband. I don't know why this is true, but I catch myself correcting him on the silliest details or arguing over something as inconsequential as whether or not we saw a movie together. Even when I realize that there is no need to prove myself, I have a hard time letting go. If you ever find yourself in this situation you might want to ask yourself which is more important, being right or being happy. As Dr. Wayne Dyer often says in his lectures, "when you have the choice to be right or be kind, choose being kind." Your ego won't want to let go, but you are guaranteed more happiness and peace if you do!

Resources:

Borysenko, Joan. (1987) Minding the Body, Mending the Mind. Bantam Books.

Borysenko, Joan and Borysenko, Miroslav. (1994) The Power of the Mind to Heal. Hay House, Incorporated.

Burns, David. (1993) Ten Days to Self-Esteem. Quill William Morrow.

Levine, Barbara Hobberman. (1991) Your Body Believes Every Word You Say. Aslan Publishing.

Chapter VI
Body Image:
In the Eye of the Beholder

I am not a body; I am free
For I am still as God created me.
(Excerpt from a prayer in <u>A Course in Miracles</u>)

When you go to the grocery store to buy a bag of frozen broccoli, do you care more about the looks of the packaging or about the quality of the broccoli? The quality of the broccoli, of course! You're not going to eat the packaging, you're going to eat the broccoli. When it comes to our bodies, it would be helpful if women would have the same attitude they do about the packaging of frozen broccoli. You definitely want the package to do its job by keeping the broccoli frozen and air tight, but you are more interested in what's inside the bag.

If you believe as I do, that our bodies are containers for our spirits, then you understand why I put less emphasis on physical appearance (unlike most "health" professionals). Yes, the body is very important, because without it your spirit would not be able to experience this world or be of service to anyone. But, the truth is, most of us spend a disproportionate amount of time and energy not only concentrating on our physical bodies - but more specifically on our own imperfections, as well as comparing and judging others.

How poor body image affects your health

When we dislike our bodies we often fail to nurture them with daily physical activity, healthy and delicious foods, rest and relaxation. I know when I am feeling good about my body I am much more likely to go for a walk, a swim, or choose the foods that will energize me. But when I'm feeling fat and dumpy, I don't want to be seen in my shorts or my bathing suit. I am much more likely to say "Oh what the heck" and order a hot fudge sundae for lunch - which only makes me feel more lethargic.

Not only do these negative thoughts affect our behaviors, they also affect our body's chemistry. If you think back to Chapter 1, you'll remember the discussion about neuropeptides, the chemicals that your body produces based on your thoughts and feelings. Well, when you chronically stress yourself by focusing on what you hate about your body, you are flooding your body with stress hormones which have a cascade of negative effects. Here are just a few of the effects of these stress hormones:

1. Inhibition of protein synthesis. (No wonder your nails and hair aren't strong)

2. Inhibition of fat metabolism. (No wonder you keep storing fat even though you've changed your diet and increased your exercise)

3. Reduction of favorable interferon levels which are necessary for certain immune cells to do their job of ridding the body of virus-infected cells and cancer cells.

Since the stress we cause ourselves, worrying about our bodies, can actually cause our bodies harm, it is really important that we women get a grip on our body image. The advertisers and fashion industry aren't going to do it for us. It will have to be an inside job.

We live with a lie in our culture that beauty is an objectively measured quality that is universally accepted and changeless. Beauty is not universal or changeless - and it definitely is not objectively measured. I've always wanted to write a book entitled Perfect 10 , which would show the ideals of beauty across cultures and across time. I have wanted to show that regardless of your size, color or shape, in some culture, during some time period, you were a perfect "10".

For example, in the matriarchal Goddess cultures from about 25,000 B.C to about 700 B.C. the situation was very different from ours. Instead of the older rich men seeking company of younger "beautiful" women, older women had several expendable youths who "serviced the divine womb". In the Nigerian Wodaabe tribe, women hold economic power and the tribe is obsessed with male beauty. Wodaabe men spend hours together in elaborate makeup sessions and compete in beauty contests (provocatively painted and dressed) judged by women (Body and Soul, Linda Villarosa). Can you imagine how different a woman's self-image would be in that culture?

Closer to home and to our time period, all you have to do is look at the previous generation. At that time, the average model weighed eight percent less than the average American woman, whereas today she weighs 23 percent less. When Twiggy appeared in Vogue magazine in 1965 her thinness, which is now commonplace, was shocking at the time. Even Vogue was tentative in her introduction explaining that "Twiggy is called Twiggy because she looks as though a strong gale would snap her in two and dash her to the ground...Twiggy is of such a meager constitution that other models stare at her. Her legs look as though she has not had enough milk as a baby and her face has that expression one feels Londoners wore in the blitz." (Beauty Myth, Naomi Wolf)

Nevertheless, the "you can never be too thin" mentality has taken women by storm. As a result, surveys in women's magazines show that 90 percent of respondents think they weigh too much. In a recent study of high school girls, 53 percent were unhappy with their bodies by age thirteen, and by age eighteen 78 percent were dissatisfied. A 1984 Glamour magazine survey of thirty-three thousand women showed that 75 percent of women aged eighteen to thirty-five believed they were fat, while only 25 percent were medically "overweight". Astonishingly, 45 percent of the underweight women thought they were fat! The same survey showed that women chose losing ten to fifteen pounds above success in work or in love as their most desired goal. (Beauty Myth, Naomi Wolf)

Often I hear women state that they want to lose 10 or 15 pounds to improve their health. This is another myth. Even according to conventional medical wisdom, weight does not become a risk factor until it exceeds 20 percent of ideal body weight. In other words, if the medical chart says your ideal weight (which in itself is an arguable standard) should be between 135 and 150 pounds, then you would have to weigh more than 180 pounds before the weight itself would be considered a health risk. Add to that the fact that the National Institutes of Health studies which linked obesity to heart disease and stroke were based on male subjects. And when a study of females was finally published in 1990, it showed that weight made only a fraction of the difference for women than it made for men. Although an extra 10 or 15 pounds may not be a significant health risk for women, the stress caused by trying to lose it is!

The 36 billion-dollar diet industry is happy to have so many women so dissatisfied with their bodies. They, along with the fashion, cosmetic, and plastic surgery industries, are the only big winners. Aside from the malnutrition that results from consistent dieting, women suffer in many ways. We expend enormous amounts of mental and emotional energy trying to change our bodies. We fail to enjoy the pleasures of strolling in the neighborhood, swimming in the ocean, or dancing at weddings for fear that we aren't the right size to be seen doing these activities. We avoid physical intimacy with our partners for fear they will be disgusted with our bodies (Dr. Marcia Germaine Hutchinson estimates that 65 percent of women do not like their bodies, and that poor physical self-esteem leads women to shy away from physical intimacy). We stay home from parties because we don't want to buy a new dress until we lose ten pounds. And the list goes on....

Menopause

Addressing menopause, fat actually serves an important function in a woman's body. A weight gain during menopause is biologically necessary. The average weight gain is about twelve pounds (<u>Why Women Need Chocolate</u>, Debra Waterhouse). Although it has not been scientifically determined exactly how much weight gain is necessary, here are two good reasons that some additional fat is important:

1. Fat is a natural source of estrogen. As your ovaries stop producing estrogen, the fat cells take over and are the primary source of estrogen production for post-menopausal women.

2. Extra weight helps lower the risk of osteoporosis. That's because your bones will increase the uptake of calcium in order to withstand the added stress of carrying a few more pounds. The only catch is that you must be moving your body in weight-bearing activity in order to garner this benefit.

The Image of Aging

Not only is it considered an unspeakable offense to have mature, rounded hips and bellies; it is also considered very poor taste to age. In other words, not only must you be thin, you must also be young. Did you know that 85 percent of fashion magazine models are under the age of 25? So when you are perusing the magazines while waiting in line at the check-out counter, it is not likely that you will be represented in the pages. What you can find (in between the pages of diet and exercise articles) are numerous advertisements for "anti-aging" products.

Dr. Ellen Langer conducted a very interesting study on aging. She took a group of male volunteers over the age of seventy to a retreat center for five days. They all agreed to live in the present as though it were 1959. Dr. Langer instructed them to dress and have conversations as if it were 1959. They had 1959 newspapers and magazines to read, Walter Cronkite on the news and Alfred Hitchcock movies to watch. They even brought pictures of themselves from that year and put them around the center.

Prior to the stay at the retreat center, Dr. Langer measured many of the parameters that often deteriorate with aging, such as physical strength, perception, cognition, taste, hearing and memory. Over the course of the five days, many of the chosen parameters actually improved. Serial photographs showed that the men looked about five years younger as well. Their hearing and memory improved, too.

As they changed their mindsets about aging, their physical bodies changed as well! Dr. Langer writes, *"The regular and irreversible cycles of aging that we witness in the later stages of human life may be a product of certain assumptions about how one is supposed to grow old. If we didn't feel compelled to carry out these limiting mindsets, we might have a greater chance of replacing years of decline with years of growth and purpose."*

"Youth is not a time of life- it is a state of mind. It is not a matter of ripe cheeks, red lips and supple knees; it is a temper of the will, a quality of the imagination, a vigor of emotions! It is a freshness of the deep springs of life.

You are as young as your faith, as old as your doubt; as young as your self-confidence, as old as your fear; as young as your hope, as old as your despair.

In the central place of your heart there is a wireless station; so long as it receives messages of beauty, hope, cheer, courage, grandeur and power, so long you are young."
General Douglas MacArthur

Shifting from Self-judgment to Self-acceptance

How do you begin to heal your self-image and stop criticizing yourself? Here is what I do, and what I have counseled thousands of women to across the country to do.

1) Do not read fashion magazines. Not only do the models not represent a realistic picture of what a REAL woman looks like, the advertisements that fill the magazine are designed to make you feel dissatisfied with yourself in some way. They want to entice you to buy a product that will "fix" your problem

2) Don't compare yourself to others.

3) Have friends of all ages and practice non-judgment *"Judgment is antithetical to peace."* Dr. Wayne Dyer, <u>Your Sacred Self</u>

4) Anytime you catch yourself making negative comments about aging, stop yourself in mid-sentence and replace the statement with something positive, even if you say it silently to yourself. For instance, recently while teaching yoga to some of my women friends I caught myself making a comment about the sagginess of my breasts. Before I could even correct my negativity one of my students said, "yes, wasn't it a wonderful blessing to be able to have nursed your baby for so long?"

5) Create an affirmation that you memorize, and repeat it over and over to yourself as often as possible - sort of like a mantra. I'll tell you mine, but I really believe it's best to make up your own. Here is mine:

> I am strong and beautiful
> Compassionate and bright
> Full of love and Full of light

Here are some of my favorite affirmations from a book by Gerald Jampolsky and Diane Cirincione called Change Your Mind, Change Your Life:

What counts in life is the fullness of my heart- not the number of wrinkles on my face.

I am never too old to make new choices.

I am never too old to learn new things or explore new ideas.

I am never too old to make a difference.

I will remember that the essence of my being is spirit and that my life is not limited to the reality of my body.

Today I will concentrate on the love I give to others rather than on my perception of our bodies.

Either use some of these affirmations or create your own. Whenever I find myself in some sort of self-loathing behavior I repeat my affirmation, aloud if possible, and I can feel a shift in my emotions. Try it. It's amazing and empowering, and will help you begin to appreciate yourself!

In addition to repeating affirmations, the other four techniques mentioned will provide you with a powerful means of breaking the cultural demands upon women to be ever young and beautiful. For a more global perspective, perhaps we might even take a familiar prayer and transform it into a universally healing affirmation. A dear friend, healer, and teacher, Dorothy Stewart, has created one from the beautiful prayer of St. Francis:

I am an instrument of Peace. Where there is hatred, I sow love. Where there is injury, I pardon. Where there is doubt, I have faith. Where there is despair, I have hope. Where there is darkness, I create light. And where there is sadness, I bring joy.

Resources:

Naomi Wolf (1992) The Beauty Myth. Anchor Books.

Linda Villarosa (1994) Body and Soul: The Black Women's Guide to Physical Health and Emotional Well-Being. HarperCollins.

Gerald Jampolsky, M.D. and Diane Cirincione (1994) Change Your Mind, Change Your Life. Bantam Books.

Chapter VII
Breathe!

As American women, we learn from an early age to suppress strong emotions. From a biological standpoint, the best way to do this is to hold our breath. Have you ever noticed that when you are trying not to laugh aloud in church or trying not to cry in front of a co-worker, you hold your breath? Add to that the cultural imperative for women to have a flat abdomen, and you have the perfect recipe for creating a society of shallow "chest breathers", rather than healthy "abdominal breathers".

Try this exercise:

1) Sit comfortably with your spine elongated.

2) Place one hand on your abdomen below your navel and the other hand on your chest.

3) Now take in a full, deep breath and pay attention to which hand moves first— chest hand or belly hand.

If the hand on your chest moved first, you are breathing like the majority of women in our society. This breath is performed by expanding and lifting the rib cage, which only fills the upper and middle portions of the lungs. This is approximately 1/7 of your lung's capacity - not much. Chest breathing is also called "stress" breathing. In order to get enough oxygen through chest breathing, your heart rate and respiratory rate must increase - which stresses your body and mind.

If the hand on your abdomen moved first you are using the diaphragm to help bring air into the lower lobes of the lungs. This is so important because there is more blood available for oxygen exchange in the lower parts of the lungs.

During inhalation, as the diaphragm contracts and flattens out, the lower rib cage expands and the abdomen feels protruded. During exhalation, the contracted diaphragm relaxes into its dome-shaped parachute position. To completely expel the breath from the lower lobes, the abdominal muscles have to engage to squeeze out the residual air (which makes breathing a wonderful abdominal muscle toning activity when done correctly).

The goal is to breathe so that the abdomen expands first and as the air rises the chest fills and then the collarbones rise. When we engage in healthy abdominal breathing, we get superb oxygen exchange, our hearts don't have to work overtime, and our blood pressure tends to remain stable.

THREE-PART BREATH: To calm and relax the body

Practicing this three-part breath is useful for your meditation practice as well as for your exercise program. It will allow you to feel both awake and relaxed while remaining calm and focused.

Part One:

1. Sit with the spine elongated

2. Exhale fully as you contract the abdominal wall and press it against your spine.

3. Inhale as the lower abdomen expands. While learning this breath it helps to place one of your hands on your lower abdomen to help you feel the movement.

4. Exhale as the lower abdomen contracts and presses against the spine.

Part Two:

1. Place your hands on either side of your rib cage at your bra line with your thumb wrapped around the back side and your fingers around the front.

2. As you inhale, feel the movement expand the rib cage and push your fingers away from each other.

3. As you exhale, feel the rib cage contract and the fingers move toward each other.

Part Three:

1. Hold the abdomen slightly inward and the rib cage stationary.

2. Breathe in and out by allowing the collarbones to move up and down.

Parts One, Two and Three Together:

1. Finally, combine all three parts. As you begin to inhale, the abdomen expands.

2. As more air enters the lungs feel the expansion ascend through the ribs and then finally allow the collarbone to float up. (Thus the three parts are lower abdomen, chest and collarbones).

3. When you begin to exhale, let the collarbones begin to fall first. Then as you continue exhaling let the chest deflate and finally the lower abdomen contracts.

4. As you practice this breath, begin to slow down both the inhalation and the exhalation.

ALTERNATE NOSTRIL BREATH:
To balance the mind

1. Hold the right hand in front of the nose.

2. Tuck the first and second fingers into your palm.

3. Extend your thumb and the fourth and fifth fingers.

4. Close the right nostril with your thumb.

5. Exhale and inhale through the left nostril.

6. Then close your left nostril with the fourth and fifth fingers and open your right.

7. Exhale and inhale through the right nostril.

8. Repeat the cycle at least five times.

9. Use the type of breathing described as "three part breathing".

10. Eventually begin making the exhalation twice as long as the inhalation.

RAPID ABDOMINAL BREATHING:
To energize mind and body

1. Sit with the spine erect.

2. Keep the neck, shoulders, and face relaxed.

3. Exhale forcible using your abdominal muscles.

4. Inhale passively by relaxing the abdominal muscles. When the abdominal muscles relax a vacuum is created which naturally pulls in air. DO NOT FORCE THE INHALATION.

5. Repeat, letting your abdomen go in and out rhythmically.

6. Begin by doing three rounds of ten breaths.

7. Add ten breaths each week until you reach 30 breaths per round.

8. Relax for 20 seconds between rounds, slowing your breathing.

9. Start with a rhythm of one breath every two seconds, gradually speeding up to two breaths every second.

*Rapid abdominal breathing should be avoided if you have hypertension or epilepsy and during menstruation or pregnancy.

If you ever feel light-headed simply stop for a moment. Since most of us use only 1/7th of the lung's capacity when we breathe we are not accustomed to the feeling of bringing so much oxygen into our system. After you have been practicing these breathing exercises for a while you will begin to reap the energizing benefits to your body and the focusing, calming benefits to your mind.

Resource:

Farhi, Donna (1996) The Breathing Book. Henny Holt.

Chapter VIII
Simplicity

" 'Tis a gift to be simple,
'Tis a gift to be free."
Old Shaker hymn

"Finding a way to live the simple life is one of life's
supreme complications."
TS Eliot

The sheer complexity of our lives causes internal distress and can wreak havoc on our bodies. Our hearts get overstimulated, our immune systems become suppressed, hormonal output becomes imbalanced and our reproductive systems no longer function normally. But because we are addicted to complexity, we can't find a way out. I know. I've been there, and I've spent the past 8 years consciously finding ways to simplify my life. In the third year of "life simplification", I became acutely aware of the positive impact this plan was having on my health. Ever since then I have been adding this component to the health education and counseling that I do. I truly believe that anyone in our culture who wants to make positive health changes must first simplify their life in order to accommodate the changes and to create peace in their minds.

"I've learned not to hold on too tightly to things in the life because it hurts too much when God has to pry my fingers away from them. Now I hold on loosely."
Corrie Ten Boom

"...poverty has a very human face-one that is different from "simplicity". Poverty is involuntary and debilitating, whereas simplicity is voluntary and enabling."
Duane Elgin

How much do we need?

Have you ever seen the house where your parents grew up in and asked, "How did you survive with that tiny bathroom? Where are the closets? How could five kids share two bedrooms?" What your parents might have called luxuries, you're probably calling necessities: walk-in closets, master bathroom suites, separate bedrooms, a phone in every room, cellular phones, home computers, televisions and VCRs. And that doesn't include the recent onslaught of other must-have 90's gadgets like espresso and cappuccino machines, bread makers, faxes and digital satellite television.

One reason for our inability to achieve simplicity is that we clutter our lives with far more things than we actually need. We buy these things we don't need, with money we don't have, to impress people we don't even know! This means that much of our leisure time is spent taking care of or paying for things we really didn't want in the first place. The problem is we've been doing it so long, we don't realize that something is amiss.

There's a story that I remember hearing as a child that illustrates how we often don't even know why we do the things we do.

One day a newly married husband watched as his wife prepared a ham for their first Thanksgiving dinner.

At one point he asked, "Sweetheart, why did you cut off both ends of the ham?"

"Because my mother always cut off the ends of the ham before baking it," she said.

"But why?"

"I don't know - let's ask her when she comes over for dinner."

So when the mother arrived the new bride asked, "When you prepared the ham every Thanksgiving, you always cut off both ends - why did you do that?"

"I learned that step by watching my mother prepare the ham," said the mother.

"But why?"

"I don't know-let's ask your grandmother when she arrives for dinner."

Finally, Grandmother arrived for dinner and had barely entered the house when both mother and daughter asked, "When you prepared the ham for baking, you always cut off both ends- why did you do that?"

"Well," Grandmother said, "the pan was too small."

Just like the young woman in the story, we become trapped by the belief that we must have certain possessions and be involved in certain activities in order to be happy and fulfilled.

"Our life is frittered away by detail. Simplify, simplify, simplify."
Henry David Thoreau

Fortunately, I have had several opportunities to experience living a very simple life. My first experience was Christmas of 1984 when I spent two weeks traveling to small villages in central Mexico with a medical missionary group. My job was to sort through the two school buses full of donated clothing and find one item to fit each person in the village as they stood in line outside the bus. There was no running water or electricity in these villages, and even the cows that wandered the streets looked hungry. But I've never seen so many joyous and generous people. These people who had virtually no material possessions seemed less anxious and worried than most North Americans. And despite the fact that they rarely had enough to feed their families, they always offered us food at the end of the day. When I returned home I was instantly struck by the waste and overindulgence of our culture. For a couple of years, I managed to keep my life simple and stay out of the "rat race" of buying more things and then working harder to pay for them. Unfortunately, the effect wore off, and soon I was just like everyone else. I had two closets full of in-season clothes (while the out-of-season clothes were stored), and I was working 10 and 12 hour days with over an hour and a half commute.

After completing my doctorate I decided to give myself a gift of a three-month sabbatical. So I stored all of my belongings and hit the road. I spent the first month at Satchidananda Ashram in Virginia and then the next in the rain forest of Costa Rica. In both places, I re-discovered that I was much more serene with fewer possessions and commitments. Upon returning, I vowed to make life simplification a priority, and have been doing it ever since.

Sure it works if you're single, but what about if you're married and have kids? In the beginning of my simplification efforts I was single. Then I married and became a stepmother. Instantly, life was twenty times more complex. But after awhile I began to see how I had bought into some of the myths of our culture again and found ways to simplify. Now, with a six-month-old baby boy added to the family, I've had to go through the whole process again. It is an endless process because our culture does not support a simplified lifestyle. Therefore, you must constantly remind yourself what you are doing and why you are doing it. When you start slowing down, cutting back, and creating time for yourself, the important things become obvious.

My goal after returning from the peacefulness of the ashram and the rainforest was to recreate that feeling without having to leave my family, my hometown and my career. I started with two books: Elaine St. James' book, Simplify Your Life, and Your Money or Your Life by Joe Dominguez and Vicki Robin. The following are suggestions that come from some of the lifestyle changes we have made as a family on our journey to create serenity in the middle of the big city.

1. Clear out the clutter.

This is self-explanatory, but let me elaborate. Everything you look at creates thoughts. So if your house, garage or closets are crammed with stuff that you don't need or use, you are constantly bombarding your mind with thoughts of confusion, displeasure, claustrophobia or irritation. The neuropeptides created from these thoughts are definitely not the ones you want flooding your body!

Getting rid of stuff you really don't need is tremendously liberating. Not only do my husband and I regularly give things to Goodwill, but our ten-year old goes through his things, too. The smallest member of the family, our 6 month- old son, probably has the largest accumulation of toys and clothes. These wonderful gifts and hand-me-downs are now shared with a friend at church who is expecting a baby in a few months. Every Sunday I have items in my trunk to give to her, as I attempt to stay clutter-free.

"To have what we want is riches, but to be able to do without is power".
George MacDonald

2. When you bring in something new, throw out some thing old.

This is an important step once you have reduced the clutter. I learned this technique from my mentor and friend, Debbie Rosas, who even applies it to her artwork. It applies to clothes, books, toys, shoes, tools, dishes, eyeglasses, linens, nail polish, everything! Get something new - get rid of something old.

3. Don't watch the 10:00 news.

Sleep is a time for your body to heal itself and rest.

It is a time for the protein you ate that day to be used in repairing tissues. But if you watch the 10:00 news, you will stay in a state of anxiety due to the content of it, and increase the amount of stress hormones being produced. The last thing on your mind when falling asleep is what you process through the night. That means your body does not rest and protein synthesis is inhibited by the production of stress hormones like corticosteroids.

If you have been in the habit of watching the 10:00 news, use the new-found time to talk with your spouse or do progressive muscle relaxation.

"There are two ways to get enough; one is to continue to accumulate more and more. The other is to desire less."
G.K Chesterton

4. Turn off the TV.

Think about what is portrayed on TV and ask yourself if it adds peace and tranquility to your life, or if it makes you feel restless, dissatisfied and fearful. You may think TV relaxes you. What you may not realize is that the constant advertising is designed to make you feel dissatisfied with yourself and your life. Therefore, you will buy products and services that will allegedly "fix" whatever isn't right.

5. Drop Call Waiting.

My mom is the one who helped me understand the importance of this one. Every time call waiting interrupted one of our conversations she would just hang up. When I called her back she would let me know that taking a call in the middle of our conversation gave her the feeling that I was too busy to talk to her. You may think that my mom was being too sensitive, but I now believe she was right to point out how rude this interruption was. Not to mention that juggling two calls on the same line at the same time definitely does not make anyone's life simpler?

If you share a home line with a business line like I do, you may not be able to drop call waiting. If that is the case, I suggest you get an automated voice messaging system so you can allow incoming calls to be answered by the message service. You can check your messages later.

6. Simplify and organize your eating habits.

In my "pre-family" days I simplified my own eating habits by eating food as close to its natural state as possible, but I didn't plan ahead. In a typical week I would go to the grocery store four or five times. Once a husband and kids entered the picture, I was forced to organize and cut down the number of trips to the grocery store. Now, I have seven basic dinners that are quick and easy to prepare as well as healthy. I sit down on Saturday or Sunday and make a list of everything I'll need to have on hand in order to make these meals. Then, I purchase them when the grocery store is least crowded. This one lifestyle change has added at least three hours a week back into my time.

7. Don't bring junk mail into the house.

I must be on 50 mailing lists. Every day my mailbox is stuffed with unheard of catalogs, special offerings from book clubs, newsletters, baby food companies, cleaning services, photography studios, you name it - it is in there. Occasionally, I'd be intrigued with a catalog item or special offer and actually order it. Now, I go straight to the large recycle bin in the kitchen and throw away unopened catalogs and envelopes that I didn't specifically request. Not only does it save time, it saves money because I don't buy unnecessary items.

One great way to decipher junk mail from important mail is to look at the postage. Separate your mail into two piles: first class postage and bulk rate postage. The first class postage pile is probably important. The bulk rate pile is probably junk.

8. Learn to meditate.

I resisted this step for quite awhile because I wasn't able to sit still. I started with walking meditations, and soon was able to sit still and focus my mind on a simple word. I am positive that meditating regularly gave me the focus and clarity to complete my dissertation.

9. Trust your intuition.

Have you ever had a "gut feeling" that told you not to do something? Most of us have. And most of us then sit down with pencil and paper to "verify" the information by making a list of pros and cons. In some cases, despite the fact that our gut feeling was "Don't do it!", the pros outweigh the cons and we decide to do it anyway. Then a month or a year down the road we say to ourselves, "I knew I shouldn't have done that!"

Try going with your gut feelings and see if it doesn't save you time - not only time saved from making end-less lists, but time saved from having to recuperate from poor decisions. Psychoneuroimmunologists say that your gut may be more accurate than your analytical mind because it hasn't learned to doubt itself!

10. Know what REALLY matters.

Do you HAVE to read the paper every day? Do the beds HAVE to be made every day? Do the sheets and towels HAVE to be washed so often? Do you HAVE to volunteer for that civic duty? Do you HAVE to read your e-mail? Usually the answer is no. Of course, we do lots of things in our lives that we don't HAVE to do - just make sure you aren't falling into the same trap as the woman who was cutting off the end of the ham. Make sure the things you do really matter. Remember, there are only 24 hours in a day - make the best of them!

11. Learn to incorporate physical activity into your normal daily routine.

In the past eight years fitness research has shown that small bouts of activity throughout the day provide the same health benefits as one extended exercise session. It may not improve your fitness level (aerobic capacity) as much, but it can help prevent many physical illnesses. It will also give you more energy. This, too, is an important part of everyday life.

12. Don't answer the phone just because it's ringing.

Boy, was this a tough one for me. Until I got mar-ried and had a son I think I was truly incapable of not answering a ringing phone. But then I began to notice that I would answer the phone just as we were beginning to read a bedtime story or right in the middle of dinner. Now, I let the messaging system answer the call, and I call back when I can give the other party my undivided attention. As Elaine St. James says, *"Just because it's convenient for them to call doesn't mean it's convenient for you to answer."*

Once you have simplified your life, it will be easier for you to see a little room in you hectic schedule, you will be able to think more clearly, accomplish the important tasks, and relax a little more.

Resources:

Elaine St. James (1995) <u>Simplify Your Life</u> .Hyperion

Joe Dominguez and Vicki Robin (1992) <u>Your Money or Your Life</u>. Penguin

Chapter IX
Meditation: Calming a Stormy Mind

"Meditation is not an evasion,
it is a serene encounter with reality."
Thich Nhat Hanh

"Meditation is the calming of the mind so we can listen
to God instead of the babbling that goes on in our heads
all day." Sister Mary McGehee

When I first sat in meditation I could not still my mind. It raced from one subject to another, while the peace that I had been told about eluded me. As the teacher guided us in meditation, he said, "if you have a thought, just notice it and then let it go." So I did - and I was appalled! My thoughts were nothing more than laundry lists, chores to do, people to call, items to purchase, and many miscellaneous wanderings.

You've already read how important I believe it is to simplify your life - and once you begin a meditation practice it will become even clearer to you. If you are like most women, your mind operates much like a computer system. You have multiple applications operating at the same time and with a click of the mouse you can switch from one application to another. That's why you are able to give a marketing presentation, while suddenly remembering that you need to buy your best friend a birthday gift and plan what you are going to wear for dinner that night. Or you can make dinner while talking on the phone, watch the baby and call out spelling words for your ten-year old - and never miss a beat! Unfortunately, this gift of "multi-tasking" can become a curse when we can't figure out how to stop the chaos in our minds and calm down.

The purpose of meditation is to help you clear the clutter from your mind so you are left with your self and your connection to God (or your higher self, Goddess, the source - whatever you choose to call it).   In one of her lectures, Dr. Gladys McGary, M.D., M.P.H. made the following analogy: If you compare yourself to a slide projector, your body is like the projector, your mind is like the slide to be projected, your spirit is like the electrical current coming through the cord and God (or whatever you call your source or higher power) is like the source of the electricity. If we keep focusing on the projector and the slide but don't have a good electrical connection, what good is the slide projector? Likewise, if we focus only on the body and mind without keeping our connection to the source, what good are we?

Mainstreaming Meditation

In his landmark book, The Relaxation Response, Dr. Herbert Benson scientifically studied the effects of meditation. He discovered that when a person meditates they elicit a relaxation response, which counteracts the negative physiological changes induced by perceived stress. Instead of calling the technique "meditation" when he introduced it in the United States, he called it "The Relaxation Response". Dr. Benson found that by practicing a simple breathing meditation people were able to improve long-term health by relieving stress.

Practicing a simple breath-focused meditation can also have a powerful impact on women's health. For instance, the results of one study showed that by practicing this simple meditation for 20 minutes a day, menopausal women who had been having symptoms of menopause experienced a 50% reduction in the frequency and intensity of hot flashes. Another study showed that by eliciting the relaxation response there was a 58% reduction of symptoms among women with severe premenstrual syndrome. This is a significant reduction, especially compared with a recent study of the effect of Prozac for PMS symptoms which showed a 52% reduction in patients taking the drug.

Following is Dr. Benson's description of the four components necessary to bring about The Relaxation Response:

1. A Quiet Environment

Ideally, you should choose a quiet, calm environment with as few distractions as possible. A quiet room is suitable, as is a place of worship. The quiet environment contributes to the effectiveness of the repeated word or phrase by making it easier to eliminate distracting thoughts.

2. A Mental Device

In preparation for The Relaxation Response one must make a shift in mental activity. To shift the mind from logical, externally oriented thought, there should be a constant stimulus: a sound, word, or phrase repeated silently or aloud, or fixed gaze at an object. Since one of the major difficulties in the elicitation of The Relaxation Response is "mind wandering", the repetition of the word or phrase is a means to break the train of distracting thoughts. If you are using a repeated sound or word, close your eyes. Of course, your eyes are open if you are gazing. Attention to the normal rhythm of breathing is also useful and enhances the repetition of the sound of the word.

3. A Passive Attitude

When distracting thoughts occur, they are to be disregarded and attention redirected to the repetition or gazing. You should not worry about how well you are performing the technique, because this may well prevent The Relaxation Response from occurring. Adopt a "let it happen" attitude. The passive attitude is perhaps the most important element in eliciting The Relaxation Response. Distracting thoughts will occur. Do not worry about them. When these thoughts do present themselves and you become aware of them, simply return to the repetition of the mental device. These other thoughts do not mean you are performing the technique incorrectly. They are to be expected.

4. A Comfortable Position

A comfortable posture is important so no undue muscular tension occurs. It is preferable to sit with the spine elongated. If you are lying down, there is a tendency to fall asleep. You should, however, be comfortable and relaxed.

Meditation Methods

There are many methods of meditation. One of the best-documented is Transcendental Meditation. When you search the medical literature, most of the studies use this form of meditation. However, tests at the Thorndike Memorial Laboratory of Harvard show that a similar technique used with any sound, phrase, prayer or mantra brings forth the same physiologic changes noted during Transcendental Meditation: decreased oxygen consumption, decreased carbon-dioxide elimination and decreased rate of breathing.

Meditation begins with concentration - trying to focus your mind on any one point. It is important to note that there are many ways to meditate, and many choices for focal points. I often say to my beginning students that there are as many ways to meditate as there are people. I have chosen a few methods to describe to you in hopes that one of them will meet your needs.

Meditation Using Breath as a Focus

1) Sit quietly in a comfortable position with your spine erect. You can sit in a chair or on the floor. If you choose a chair, it is best to use a straight-backed one and sit with the spine away from the chair back.

2) Close your eyes.

3) Deeply relax all your muscles, beginning at your feet and progressing up to your face. Keep them relaxed.

4) Breathe through your nose and become aware of your breathing. As you breathe in and out, feel the breath

come and go. Keep full awareness on the breath without changing its pattern. Simply notice it as it moves through your body.

5) Continue for 10 - 20 minutes. You may open your eyes to check the time, but do not use a loud, buzzing alarm. If you want to use an alarm, have it set for soft music so it does not startle you. When you finish, sit quietly for several minutes. At first, keep your eyes closed and then slowly open them. Do not stand up for a few minutes.

6) Do not worry whether you are successful in achieving a deep level of relaxation. Maintain a passive attitude and permit relaxation to occur at its own pace. When distracting thoughts occur, try to ignore them by not dwelling upon them and returning to the focus of the breath. Practice the technique once or twice daily. However, avoid meditating within two hours after a meal since the digestive processes seem to interfere with the ability to sit and meditate.

Meditation using repetition of a mantra, a word, or a prayer

For many people, the breath is not enough to keep their mind from wandering excessively, so they choose to focus on a mantra, a word or a prayer. A mantra is a sound vibration, mystical in nature, which is said to align the mind, body and spirit - to create harmony. Through generations of spiritual masters, mantras have been handed down to students seeking spiritual enlightenment. By constantly repeating them you produce certain vibrations within you and throughout your physical, emotional and intellectual self.

The reason I particularly like using a mantra is that it has no meaning in English, so it doesn't encourage "story telling" in my mind. However, if you do not have access to a spiritual master then you might simply choose a word or a prayer to repeat. My only suggestion is that whatever you choose, make it spiritually uplifting, and avoid something that will encourage your mind to wander. For instance, if you choose the word "peace" and find that the word makes your mind think of war, then you might need to find another word.

Once you have chosen your focus, follow the instructions for the Breath Focus Meditation. Instead of focusing on breath, you will be focusing on your mantra, word or prayer.

Walking Meditation

Slow, mindful walking is another wonderful way to experience the benefits and the spiritual connection of meditation. In fact, as a beginner meditator at the ashram, I had such a hard time sitting still, I could barely stick with it. Then the option of walking meditation was introduced to us. The slow walking and mindful breathing anchored my mind and gradually helped me learn to release the uncontrollable wanderings of my thoughts. After a month of practicing walking meditation I was able to enjoy sitting meditation, too, and now I choose my meditation technique depending on where I am. For instance, I recently spoke at a conference in Clearwater, Florida. I had a choice of doing a sitting meditation in my tiny hotel room or a walking meditation on the beach. Of course, the walking meditation won hands down!

To begin using walking as a formal meditation practice try following these guidelines:

1. Decide ahead of time how long you will do your walking meditation. (10 - 20 minutes is a good amount of time)

2. Choose a place where you can walk slowly back and forth or in a wide circle. This place should be free of distractions like noises, people or vehicles. At the ashram, we would follow the path around the meditation temple or walk the labyrinth. You may even be fortunate enough to have a church, synagogue or temple in your town that has a labyrinth to walk. A labyrinth is a single-path maze. One of the most famous labyrinths is found in the cathedral in Chartres, France.

3. Choose your focus. You can focus on your breath, a word, a sound, a prayer or an aspect of your walking.

4. If you are focusing on an aspect of your walking it is a good idea to focus your attention on one aspect rather than continuously changing.

5. Choose a pace that maximizes your ability to pay attention to your chosen focus.

All of these meditation practices are simple - but not easy. I find it harder to keep my meditation practice than any other lifestyle habit. Isn't it interesting that the hardest thing to do is sit and do nothing? Whatever you do, don't give up just because it is difficult. I assure you the benefits are well worth the effort.

Resources:

Jon Kabat-Zinn (1992) <u>Wherever You Go There You Are:</u>
<u>Mindfulness Meditation in Everyday Life</u>. Hyperion.

Benson, Herbert (1975) <u>The Relaxation Response.</u>
Wings Books.

(Plus all of the yoga books listed at the end of Chapter 3.)

Chapter X
Daily Massage:
The Healing Power of Touch

The concept of daily massage conjures up the image of extremely wealthy or famous people who can afford this luxury. But massage doesn't have to be expensive or time consuming. In fact, it doesn't even require a massage therapist. You can do it yourself just before you shower or bathe - and it only takes 5 - 10 minutes.

The benefits of doing a daily massage are many: it improves circulation of blood and lymph, it promotes flexibility of the muscles, connective tissues and joints, and it promotes softness and luster of the skin. Many studies suggest that touch and massage can enhance the body's ability to heal itself. For instance, a study presented in the Pediatrics Journal compared preterm babies who were stroked for three ten-minute periods a day for ten days to those who were not stroked. The babies who were stroked gained an average of 47% more weight per day, were more active and alert, showed more mature behaviors, and left the hospital an average of six days earlier.

Massage is not for babies only. It is important for everyone. Many people find that this massage invigorates and energizes them. Therefore, it is recommended that you do this technique in the morning. In addition to the increased energy, massaging or brushing the body assists in the elimination of toxins. By eliminating toxins through the skin you reduce the work required of your internal organs and allow your body to find balance more easily. Stimulating the lymphatic and circulatory systems increases the flow of nutrients through the body's systems, thus enhancing health, reducing stress, increasing body tone and reducing cellulite.

I mention cellulite because so many women ask me for ways to get rid of it. A word about cellulite: cellulite is not a different kind of fat. It's lumpiness is caused by the connective tissue which pulls the skin the same way stitching pulls the top layer of a quilt. It is natural for women to have cellulite. Even the thinnest models have it. Although the appearance of cellulite will decrease when you combine good nutrition, water intake and exercise with daily body brushing or massage - remember that it is normal for women to have cellulite.

How to perform daily self-massage

Warm a small amount of the oil of your choice and pour a tablespoon of the oil into your scalp. Using mainly the flat of your hand, massage the oil in vigorously as if your were washing your hair. Cover the entire scalp.
As you massage the body, add oil as needed. Move to the face and ears, massaging more gently. Gently massage the temples and backs of the ears with your fingertips. Using both the flat of the hand and the fingers, massage a small amount of oil onto your neck - front and back, and then your shoulders.

Vigorously massage your arms. Use a circular motion at the shoulders and elbows, and long back-and-forth motions on the upper arms and forearms.

Avoid being excessively vigorous on the trunk of your body. Using large, gentle circular motions, massage your chest, stomach and lower abdomen. Move your hands in a clockwise motion - up the right side, across the middle and down the left side. Use a straight up-and-down motion over the breastbone. After applying a bit of oil to both hands, gently reach around to massage the back and spine as best you can. Use an up-and-down motion.

As with the arms, vigorously massage your legs with a circular motion at the ankles and knees, straight up-and-down on the long parts. Massage your feet. Be sure to pay attention to your toes as well as the sole of each foot. If possible, leave the oil on your skin for awhile before bathing or showering.

What kind of oil should I use?

According to Ayurveda, oils may be chosen based on body type. The questionnaire you filled out in Chapter Two will help you determine which oil to use. If you are dominant Air, use heave warm oils such as sesame or almond. If you purchase oil from an Ayurvedic supply store or catalog, choose the oil for Vata. If you are dominant Fire, use cooling oils such as coconut and olive or choose an oil for Pitta from an Ayurvedic supply store or catalog. If you are dominant Earth, use lighter oils such as safflower, sunflower or mustard or choose an oil for Kapha from an Ayurvedic supply store or catalog. A dry massage using a silk glove is also beneficial for the person with Earth-dominant nature.

Massage has so many benefits. It improves circulation, helps prevent varicose veins, enhances immune function, creates glowing skin by sloughing dead skin cells from the surface and can either relax or invigorate you depending on your intention and your needs. Massaging the skin also increases production of vasoacitive intestinal polypeptide - VIP for short. VIP is the body's natural vasodilator. This means that it has the effect of lowering blood pressure - yet another benefit of massage. With so many benefits, I hope you are enticed to give self-massage a try!

Resources:

Chopra, Deepak (1991) Perfect Health. Harmony Books

Frawley, David (1990) Ayurvedic Healing. Passage Press.

Frawley, David, and Lad, Vasant (1986) The Yoga of Herbs. Lotus Presss.

Lad, Vasant (1984) Ayurveda: TheScience of Self-Healing. Lotus Press.

Lonsdorf, Nance; Butler, Veronica, and Brown, Melanie (1995) A Woman's Best Medicine: Health Happiness, and Long Life Through Ayur-Veda. Tarcher.

About the Photographer:

Marianne Howard is a Dallas-based artist, photographer, writer, conservationist and principal of IMAGEQUEST. Her photographs appear in books and magazines and her mixed media paintings are held in private collections internationally. Marianne is the founder of The International Federation of Women in Wildlife and The Women In Wildlife Foundation. The WIWF is a fund-raising organization designed to distribute funds on a global basis, through a grants process, to existing non- profit wildlife service organizations. For more information about WIWF contact Marianne at HOWARD11@msn.com

About the Editors:

Paula Murphy received her degree from the A.Q. Miller School of Journalism and Mass Communications at Kansas State University. She is currently with the Northeast Texas Chapter of the Cystic Fibrosis Foundation, and she is the founder and principal of Murphy-Walter Public Relations. Paula took her first Nia and Yoga classes from Dr. Kern in 1995. She loves hiking and backcountry camping, and she plays basketball with a ferocity that belies her "Earthy" nature.

Jessica Hall Perez has been a professional in the fitness and wellness field for fourteen years - from teaching traditional aerobics, to personal training, to managing a fitness center. Currently, she is an adjunct staff member at the Cooper Institute for Aerobics Research. She is also completing her Masters in Community Health at Texas Woman's University, where women and alternative health are her passions of study. Jessica is a White Belt Nia teacher and a believer in holistic fitness. Through movement and transformation, Jessica has discovered the importance of balancing her Air and Fire nature. It was her "Fire" nature that gave her the perseverance to edit the final draft of this book.

Deborah Kern, Ph.D. is an internationally acclaimed speaker and author on the topic of the mind/body connection in health. She integrates her training in professional fields such as nursing, business, preventive medicine and health education with her experience as a competitive race walker, yoga practitioner and personal trainer to formulate a truly unique mind/body wellness philosophy. She utilizes both Eastern and Western health and preventive techniques in a fun and informative way to assist women in making positive changes.

Dr. Kern holds a Masters in Business Administration from the University of Texas and a doctorate in Health Sciences from Texas Woman's University. She is a Black Belt Nia Trainer and yoga instructor. She presents keynote addresses and conducts workshops and seminars on the topics of mind/body connection, women's health, life simplification, holistic approaches to fitness, and breaking the cycle of stress. To contact her for speaking engagements, please call the National Wellness Speakers Bureau at 1-800-543-0583. To inquire about her training in the Nia Technique or to order audiocassettes, call 817-991-5835 or visit her website at www.DeborahKern.com

Available audiocassettes by Dr. Deborah Kern:

Beginner Hatha Yoga: Easy-to-follow voice instruction of very gentle yoga stretches with soothing background music.

Morning Meditation/Bedtime Relaxation: Designed to be kept in a cassette player at your bedside to guide you through a meditation in the morning and progressive relaxation at bedtime.

Everyday Wellness for Women: A live presentation given by Dr. Kern for a women's health event.